CROSSED PATHS

DESPERATION SQUAD
AND THE AGE OF FORTUITISM

KEVIN AUSMUS

Crossed Paths: Desperation Squad and the Age of Fortuitism by Kevin Ausmus

ISBN: 978-1-938349-14-0
Library of Congress Control Number: 2015935950

Copyright © 2015 Kevin Ausmus

This work is licensed under the Creative Commons Attribution-NonCommercial-NoDerivs 3.0 Unported License. To view a copy of this license, visit http://creativecommons.org/licenses/by-nc-nd/3.0/.

The views and opinions expressed in this book are based on the recollections and views of the author. The manufacture and presentation of this book does not warrant the accuracy, reliability, currency, or completeness of those views or statements. No liability whatsoever is assumed arising from any reliance on the views, statements and subject matter of this book.

Front Cover

- *top photo of Mr. P at the Wckr Spgt tribute show 2010 by Andy Whitson*
- *untitled painting by Bob Jones, 74 by 33 in., acrylic on found panel, 2014*
- *SX70 photo from Arts Building, 1984, photo by Art DiLion*
- *Panda Man photo by Dylan Skrah, manipulation by Kevin Ausmus*

Back Cover

- *SX70 photo of Mr. P at the PVA by Dave Alvin, 1986*

Photo of Courtney Love © Bob Gruen / www.bobgruen.com

Layout and design by Mark Givens

For information: Pelekinesis, 112 Harvard Ave #65, Claremont, CA 91711
First Pelekinesis Printing 2015

www.pelekinesis.com

Crossed Paths:

Desperation Squad and the Age of Fortuitism

Kevin Ausmus

Crossed Paths could not exist without the contributions of dozens of talented photographers, writers and artists, many of whom we would like to acknowledge. Unfortunately, some photos and fliers must go uncredited, as their authorship has been lost over time.

Bob Gruen, Fredrik Nilsen, Rog Franklin, Scott Olson, Edward Colver, Sandy B, Martin Kauper, Loren Wallachy Allen, Bruce Watkins, Rod Curtis, Art DiLion, Walt Weis, Rebecca Hamm, Dave Alvin, M.J. Stevens, John Bender, Esther Kaplan, Donna Scriven, Vic Vinson, Dawn Schultze, Ted Kovach, Karen Fox, Mark Durian, Nori Murphy Barajas, Catherine Guffey, Allen Wrench, John Ausmus, Jose Marin, Alister McDonald, Laura Kovach Cormack, Steve Cormack, Robert Jones, Sue Lawler, Brian Biddulph, John Perry, Andy Whitson, Kayleigh Skajem, Waleed Rashidi, Orlando Pina, Kevin Bronson, Catherine Jeanette, Jacqueline Vrooman, Brigitte Garney, Megan McDermott, Alex Lopes, Tyler Thorpe, Dylan Skrah, Darlene Lacey, Mark Givens, Charles Garcia, Pat Bacich, Richard Bruland, Chuck Sperry, Rolo Castillo, Stoo Odom, Craig Gleason, Hank Tracy, Melinda Lewis, Nathan Solis, Billy Cavezza, Jeff Niesel, Phil Fuller, Mike Mitino, Joseph Firman, Shelly da Cuhna, Arion Berger, Taylor Mayeda, Janet Dominick, Jim Washburn, David Carpenter, Jerry O'Sullivan, Joel Huschle, Dan Horgan, David Fondler, Mike Ward, Garey Holt, Katherine Turman, Sandra Barrera, Hazel-Dawn Dumpert, Barbara Goldman, Joshua Sanchez, Jon Jandoc, Lindsey Cash, Joe Piasecki, Kevin Mazur, Christopher Lopez, Kayne Cho, Erin Caruso, Bob Calhoun, Eddie Gonzales, Steve Jones, Jay Lansford, Mike Jones, Mike Finn, Jerry Crowe, Erin Robinson, Curt Sautter, Rob Smith, Roy Zimpel, Mike Gonzales, Brian Gittings, Steve Santamaria, Bernie Larsen, Terry Dwyer, Joey Maramba, Jon Crawford, Bob Fritz, Tim Kirk, the other Tim Kirk, and Katie Daily.

Special thanks to the following people who have helped bring Crossed Paths to life: Nicole Frazer, who first recognized the show's potential and whose drive and enthusiasm got the ball rock and rolling; Christina Franco-Long, owner of Space Gallery, who readily agreed to host the show and has provided tremendous support; Steve Lossing, whose artistic talents have been indispensable and Mark Givens, who helped shape the concept of Fortuitism and without whom there would likely have been no project and certainly no book.

I always knew that I loved the band and everyone in it, but it took preparing the Crossed Paths show and book to realize just how much I love them and how there would be no Desperation Squad without them and very possibly no joy in my life. Special special thanks to Alan Waddington, Jeff Hayes, Robert Jones, Tim Allyn, Laura Kovach, Ian Carlson, Rebecca Hamm, Caroline Dourley, Elaine Donaldson, Mark Givens, Dave Carpenter, Damon Shotwell, Dan Scratch, John Paul Maramba, Caroline Collins, Nicole Frazer and Vidal Lepe.

This book is dedicated to my family - my parents Gene and Lila Ausmus and oldest brother Regi Ausmus, all sadly passed; my brother John Ausmus, my sister Ginger Ver Halen, and my nieces Amber Long and Elizabeth Ausmus, as well as spouses Brenda Ausmus, Chris Ver Halen and Omar Long. You never really knew what I was doing all these years. Now you know.

And to Dawn Schultze, who did know what I was doing, and loved it. And I love you.

It's a short stretch of road, barely more than a half-mile, bustling with the visible vestiges of commerce: music venues, art galleries, restaurants, retail shops, even a university. However, there's an arcane secret about 2nd St. in Pomona. It's where civic policy and conceptual art met in a most unexpected, spectacular fashion and changed the course of a city forever, even as the act itself and its perpetrators have remained puzzlingly closeted, disregarded and remanded to the dustbins of history.

The campaign of the Rock and Roll Mayor in early 1993 blurred so many lines - art, music, politics, improv comedy - that to even recognize it as art requires a re-examination of what constitutes success and failure. At the heart of this puzzle is a band with a dream to conquer the world and, instead, got the plug pulled on them, kicked off the bus and voted off the program. Yet every one of these stumbles can be considered a masterpiece. And, once upon a time, they stood right where you are now and rehearsed their craft.

Desperation Squad emerged from the highly charged, long forgotten early 80s Pomona punk rock underground to become one of the most uncompromising rock acts of all time. Their live performances, whether locally, on the Warped Tour, or on national television, are the stuff of legend. Their command of the hysterically absurd has produced for them an unrivaled songbook and a genial yet perverse mascot in the Panda Man. And their tenacity and persistence provide an inspiring template for others to follow, if they themselves believe the exhortation:

"Don't ever give up on your dream!"

A 'Lil' Getogether with

DesParation squad

A FREE CONCERT
SAT. MAY 19 6:30 PM
at SAV-ON
Parking lot
on Foothill near Towne

P.A. Sound provided by
STYLE's
A FINE MUSIC STORE

Desperation Squad is the prototypical band that "never made it" and the stereotypical band that should have packed it in, before age and ambivalence colluded to produce a regretful conclusion. Perhaps.

It is possible, however, that rock and roll needed at least one terminally neglected unit to survive, albeit bloodied and bruised, to demonstrate that bands (and artists in general) should not be judged on what they didn't accomplish, based on someone else's out-sized expectations. "Unintended consequences" need not be a trope applied solely to geopolitical conflict. It happens in art all the time.

What makes rock and roll so enduring and remarkable is the egalitarian spirit engendered in its performances, the virtual guarantee that any band playing on any night can, with no regard whatsoever to their overall skill level, be the greatest rock band of all time at that particular moment. The blowback to this fitful delirium, however, is swift and brutal. By the time one opens their eyes the next day (providing they are able to), they have already been marginalized into the most useless bum on the planet, completely unable to communicate their triumph in any meaningful form that doesn't produce shrugged shoulders and rolled eyes.

That's okay if you're only in it for the short term but most bands don't get the memo. It's hard enough to keep a band together one month, let alone one year, let alone long enough to produce anything close to a legacy. No matter who passes through the process level-headed enough to get when the getting is good, there are ample fools who embrace the crazy notion that greatness can be attained, no matter how many rotting carcasses lying on the side of the road - representing every manner of can't-miss prospect, overhyped buzz, or genius inspiration (the saddest place to find broken dreams is the 25-cent CD bin) - that have to be stepped over on the journey to the Gilded Palace of Sin or whatever appropriate moniker you adopt for success in the music industry.

Perspective. Consider two starkly different appraisals to this straightforward statement - "We once opened for the Red Hot Chili Peppers!" One: "Wow! Really? That's fucking awesome!" The other: "So? I hung out with Anthony Kiedis at the Edward Hopper opening three weeks ago!" One person's greatest thrill ever is another person's invitation for snide dismissal. When you contemplate that the Rolling Stones - The Rolling Stones! - are repeatedly derided for the audacity of merely continuing to exist, you can imagine the obstacles facing any band that's not The Greatest Rock Band of All Time to evince effectively what makes them memorable and relevant.

Desperation Squad emerged from the Pomona punk rock underground by way of the Mt. Sac cultural nexus. The goal from the beginning was always be Famous Rock Stars, touring the world and selling millions of records. To which the band failed exceedingly. Conversely, the idea of producing a lifetime of obscure impossible-to-define conceptual art masterworks was never discussed, let alone pursued. Call it lucky, call it accidental, call it fortuitous. It is what it is.

Which just goes to show you. **You can't judge a band on what they have *not* accomplished, only on what they *have*.**

Diamond Bar

If you grew up in the North end of Diamond Bar in the 60s and 70s, you knew Pomona. It's presence loomed large. You went to school in Pomona, you worked in Pomona, you hung out in Pomona. Pomona was in your DNA.

If you lived in Diamond Bar in the late 70s you likely were a fan of the band Stratus, knew a hippy or two from the Gordon House, went to Mt. Sac on one pretext or another that had nothing to do with education, or even listened to a college DJ named Mr. P.

Kevin Ausmus moved to Diamond Bar with his family in 1966, suffered through a suitably painful angst-ridden junior high and arrived at Ganesha High in Pomona a newly crowned stoner with very few friends, immensely talented yet socially misdirected, cool enough to hang out with the big kids but at school cut a bizarre figure – a tippy toe gait, impenetrable stone-faced demeanor, bad skin, and wild unkempt hair.

Such was the fate of the future Mr. P when he started associating with **the neighborhood hipsters who called themselves the "Gorillas"** – in essence the lovable stoners – wickedly funny and surprisingly popular for how edgy and drug-oriented they were. The Gorillas weren't a gang as much as they were a collective – wildly creative and diverse and more than willing to take a chance on Ausmus, whom they dubbed simply "Mus." They let him hang as much as he wanted and eventually cool would rub off on him, due mainly to the presence of the Gorillas most dynamic and charming members,

12

Alan Waddington and Rob Stahl, whose special talent was making whoever they were with as cool as they were. Mus made sure he was with Alan and Rob a lot.

Alan was a musical prodigy, a non-stop stick pounding drum god, thoroughly captivating. With his older brother Brian they helped to unlock the Mus inner rock star. Kevin had been writing songs for years, scratching the lyrics down on pieces of paper and playing the tunes over and over in his head. His earliest songs reflected the introverted fantastical worlds he inhabited, hopeful and twisted. After entering Lorbeer Junior High, his songs took a much darker, almost desperate turn. The Gorillas got Mus his groove back, made him believe the little showmaker of his youth might actually fit in. Alan, Brian and Rob always prodded Mus to reach beyond the obvious, seek some kind of oddball image or thought, do something with that.

The Gorillas challenged his musical tastes. Kevin grew up on Top 40, then attended the California Jam in 1974, exposing him early on to rock and roll excess. His older brothers, however, managed to chase him away from the mainstream AOR of Led Zeppelin and Aerosmith into more bluesy territory, Allman Bros. and Little Feat, although he showed a particular shine to 70s Kinks, Neil Young and Ziggy Stardust. The Gorillas counter-offered with challenging music of King Crimson, Roxy Music and Eno. Then, just two months before high school  graduation, Brian suggested he buy a ticket to see Iggy Pop, who had just released his comeback LP "The Idiot" and was playing at the Santa Monica Civic. At that show, Mus met a fellow student from Ganesha, Jill Emery, then a freshman.

If anybody was going to get a scene going, it was Alan Waddington, whose magnetic personality and musical acumen were practically scene-builders on their own. When Alan joined the local party band Stratus, entire worlds were formed that still spin to this day.

Stratus bassist and lead singer Rod Curtis, from Diamond Bar, and guitarist/vocalist Bruce Watkins, from the Westmont section of Pomona, both graduated from Ganesha High School with Alan. Lead guitarist Craig Herring was out of Walnut.

Starting modestly, at Pomona roadhouse dives like Walter Mittys and The Connection, Stratus built an almost cult-like following in the tightly-knit Pomona/Diamond Bar area. In 1978, there were so few bands on the local circuit, Stratus would often gig at the same bar four nights a week, each night consisting of three one-hour sets of mostly rock covers - Aerosmith, Cheap Trick, "Tush" - and maybe an original if they could squeeze it in. Stratus also gigged frequently at Gazzarri's on

the Sunset Strip, and other oddball clubs like The Rock in Van Nuys and the Cuckoo's Nest in Newport Beach.

What made Stratus rock kings for all the San Gabriel Valley was their reputation as house party killers. Backyard keg parties were the primary social activity for Diamond Bar/Pomona kids at that time. Stratus ruled the roost, parties they rocked were guaranteed to attract too many kids illegally consuming mind-blowing amounts of alcohol and weed, finally getting shut down by the cops. If your house somehow didn't get trashed in the process, it was a bonus.

When reputation and word of mouth were all that was needed to attract hundreds of horny kids ready to rage - at a moment's notice - Stratus was the go-to band.

This regional stature was only enhanced by the introduction of the notorious apartment G5, a horror show bachelor pad in north Pomona that housed at various times Alan and Brian Waddington, Bruce Watkins, and Mus. G5 became the Gorilla hub, a creative living vortex where the abnormal was expected. Instead of a couch, salon-sized hair dryers greeted visitors. Alan slept on a mat in what should have been the dining room. Trash piled up like snow during a nasty New England nor'easter. Cockroaches. G5 was not for the weak of heart. Over time, G5

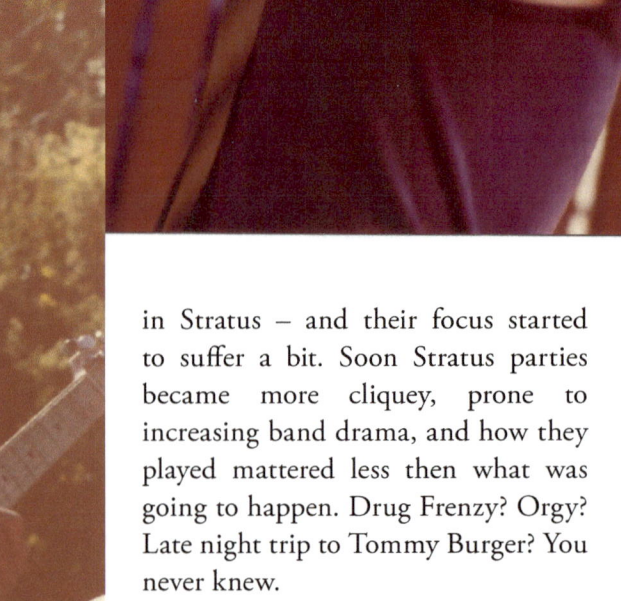

would directly tie into nearly every Ausmus/Waddington band that emerged in the 80s. Stratus were the first ones in, the trailblazers.

Watkins' arrival at G5 triggered a turning point, where Stratus took their first steps into rock and roll excess. Suffice to say, youthful proclivities, combined with the carte blanche afforded as a rock and roll band – abounded unfettered in Stratus – and their focus started to suffer a bit. Soon Stratus parties became more cliquey, prone to increasing band drama, and how they played mattered less then what was going to happen. Drug Frenzy? Orgy? Late night trip to Tommy Burger? You never knew.

"Progressive" was a band buzzword of the day, used not as a musical term, but rather to ascribe grateful awe for superior talents. "I liked that movie, it was very progressive." Rod Curtis, assessing this long-haired unkempt diamond-in-the-rough, this MUS, one day proclaimed him "Mr. Progressive", or simply, "**Mr. P.**"

An identity was born.

Mr. P existed in a number of fantasy worlds — superstar baseball player, child actor, rock star – but his real passion was listening to Top 40 DJs work their craft. This admiration and yearning only intensified with the explosion of FM radio. Being a professional athlete or musician was clearly beyond Mr. P's capabilities but, thanks to a deep booming voice and quick wit, a career in radio was thoroughly plausible. Playing rock and roll was Alan Waddington's gig. Spinning tunes and promoting new music would be Mr. P's domain. Throughout high school Mr. P was enraptured by L.A.-based DJs like Steven Clean, Shadoe Stevens, Jimmy Rabbit and Dr. Demento. He was fanatical about the Firesign Theatre, the psychedelic comedy group whose druggy mindblowing LP's would be used to good effect once Mr. P arrived at the Mt. San Antonio College radio station, 90.1 KSAK.

Mr. P found navigating his way around the already entrenched laid-back mainstream AOR hierarchy at KSAK difficult and his sense-of-humor too "out there" for the likes of KSAK management figures like Phil Markell, the blind and bitter GM who would act as Mr. P's Professor Moriarty for the next several years. Regardless, Mr. P approached even 5-minute news- and sportscasts with enthusiasm and aligned

himself with the other rookies like Jim Nelson (Fryin' Mick Rion) and Kevin Butler (Major Moon), as well as Joe Faraci, a.k.a. "Jumpin' Joe Gonzo", who just happened to be lead singer of Prisoner, a principal rival of Stratus.

Mr. P was eager to get a coveted three-hour radio shift so he could start breaking all the new punk rock/ new wave music now available. However, Markell and his cronies were dyed-in-the-wool Bob Seger "ramblin'" DJ's and bristled at the likes of not just the Sex Pistols (completely off limits) but also Talking Heads, Mr. P's new favorite band (too weird). Finally, the executive decision to keep KSAK broadcasting 24 hours a day on the weekend was Mr. P's ticket to a regular spot. In summer 1979, he acquired the Fri/Sat/Sun 3-6 a.m. graveyard shift, a time slot that virtually guaranteed he could play and say whatever he wanted. What followed was a long summer of Stratus parties, basketball games, hanging out at the beach and the slowly emerging creative persona of Mr. P, who was certain widespread fame and fortune was on the horizon.

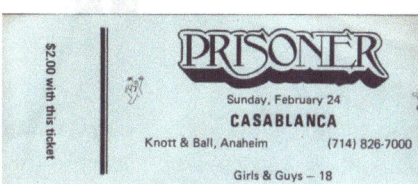

On the other side of the Mt. Sac campus, a completely different scene was going down. Nettie Lynch's poetry class was home to Brian and Alan's younger sister Darlene, who was finding her own creative footing and set of nurturing friends. The broadcasting and poetry classes were like oil and water. You couldn't mix them. Or could you?

When punk rock arrived, it was Alan who called the shot. If the Gorillas were going to have a punk rock band, and they assuredly were going to, it was going to be called **Nixon's Revenge**. The first Nixon's Revenge line-up was Alan on drums, Rob Stahl on guitar and Mr. P on harmonica and vocals. The three gathered for an improvised jam in Alan's bedroom in front of Jeff Boghosin and Dena Lack, but otherwise, Nixon's Revenge remained a conceptual band that seemingly existed merely to badger and annoy Stratus who, though greatly admired, represented the commercial corporate structure that punk rock was obliged to tear apart at the seams. Bruce Watkins, especially, was an easy target because of his proximity to Alan and Mr. P by virtue of living at G5, and his desire to explore his own punkiness, an avocation the others found easy to mock. The phrase "If Nixon's Revenge played a gig…" was voiced repeatedly as Mr. P, Alan or Brian constantly brought forth a multitude of patently absurd song ideas that Watkins retorted were "all talk".

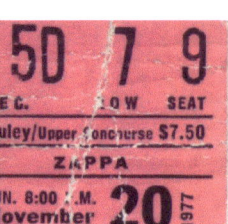

Nixon's Revenge indeed talked a good game but its implementation was a thorny logistical mess. For starters, Alan had no interest in playing drums in the band, preferring bass guitar. The two guitarists, Brian and Rob, barely knew how to play. Mr. P wrote songs but couldn't play a musical instrument. Their saxophonist, Keith Misumi, knew exactly one riff, which he could play over and over again. Even by punk rock's rather lenient musical standards, Nixon's Revenge had almost nothing in the tank but moxie. Two incidents worked to move things in the right direction.

Brian Waddington had always been the Gorillas most influential culture connoisseur, imploring Mr. P to check out the likes of Iggy Pop or Captain Beefheart. When Brian decided it was time to head out to Hollywood to check out some place called the Masque, Mr. P was eager to see his first punk rock concert.

The line-up was stellar - The Germs, Dead Kennedys, Rotters, all of which had gained notoriety. At this particular moment in L.A. punk, shows were chaotic and strange but not inherently violent or hateful. Mr. P with hair down to his butt and a bright red batting helmet, felt liberated and ran right to the front when the Dead Kennedys stepped on stage. He was greeted by Jello Biafra, who immediately grabbed the helmet and hurled it clear across the other side of the room. (The helmet would reappear at the end of the night and go on to play a minor role in the creation of D-Squad).

Well before this, the opening band, the unheralded Red Army from Phoenix, had provided all of the inspiration Nixon's Revenge would need. Starting with a super-hyper, likely meth-ed up bass player exhorting the crowd to "form a band!" to the truly bizarre conclusion of Red Army leaving the stage only to come back after kicking their lead singer out of the band *during the gig* left a powerful impression on Mr. P, who left the Masque realizing that even musical no-talents like himself could, in theory, be a vital part of the rock and roll scene.

The other incident can trace its roots to the 1978 Angels. Mr. P had been a long suffering Angels baseball fan for years, with no one to share his enthusiasm or misery. The Gorillas were stoner/athletes par excellence. Mr. P and Brian decided to attend the Angels season opener. The score was tied at 0-0 when a seldom-used journeyman catcher named Terry Humphrey came up to

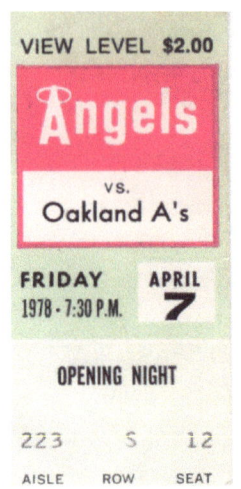

bat and smacked a triple. Humphrey scored what would turn into the winning run in a 1-0 Angels victory, making Humphrey an instant Gorilla hero. It wasn't until the next year, however, after Mr. P had decided to resume his baseball card collection, that the full impact of that game was felt. Upon inspecting the Terry Humphrey card, it was revealed his game-winning triple was his only career triple in the major leagues. For Mr. P, this was the creative revelation he needed to write his first Nixon's Revenge song, titled appropriately "Humphrey's Triple", which detailed the unlikely heroics of the season opener.

During the long summer of '79, where Mr. P went to dozens of Angels games, the music for Humphrey's Triple became centered around the stinging organ riffs played by Anaheim Stadium keyboardist Shay Torrent. Mr. P had by this point resumed writing songs, almost all of which revolved around teen angst and the low self-esteem of a kid who couldn't get laid, to a most embarrassing extent. With "Humphrey's Triple" Mr. P discovered his niche - quirky, funny slices of life with a pop flavor. With encouragement from Alan and Brian, Mr. P slowly incorporated humor and occasional pathos into his new material. It would be years before Mr. P could apply this technique to personal love songs. But his initial efforts "Humphrey's Triple" "Rerun Heaven" and "We Don't Need Watkins" had potential. They just needed an outlet.

Glass Arts of California was a factory in the City of Industry.

Brian Waddington scored a job there as some kind of warehouse supervisor, and hired Craig Herring, Bruce Watkins and Joe Gonzo to come in the mornings to manually place screws in clocks. Eventually, Mr. P was hired for the afternoon shift at which point the needling of Watkins for his punk rock shortcomings intensified, as Brian and Mr. P had all afternoon to knock around song ideas and theoretical band scenarios.

One day, Joe Gonzo arrived at Glass Arts with an offer they couldn't refuse - his band **Prisoner** had a gig lined up that weekend, the Mt. Sac Track Club Dance. How about Nixon's Revenge coming up during one of their 15-minute breaks and doing a set? Alan, Brian and Mr. P, along with Rob, Keith Misumi and bassist Paul Peterson (who would play drums) assembled the night before and cobbled together a 5-song set. "Rerun Heaven" "The Club" "Illegal Alien" "We Don't Need Watkins" and "Pam Slam" comprised the unapologetically confrontational set.

Oct. 8, 1979

This is to officially recognize that Bruce Watkins, assemblyman of Glass Arts has established a new production performance record and is commended for his outstanding performance. We sincerely hope our other employees will strive to maintain such a prodigious effort as Mr. Watkins has established. By producing 260 clips in a four hour period, we at Glass Arts feel that a written commendation is in order and are strongly considering giving Mr. Watkins a $1.00/hour raise in pay.

Thanks for a job well done.

A synthesizer player was added at the last minute, as were Darlene Waddington and her best friend Donna Stevens - not to sing or play, just to merely be on stage and act weird.

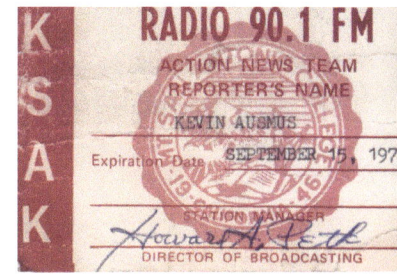

Nixon's Revenge made its long-awaited debut, in front of a few Stratus fans, some KSAK DJs, and a host of stunned and outraged Mt. Sac Track Club dance guests, including the track coach, who stormed over and attempted

to shut off the sound board (all he did was disable the tape recorder). By Nixon's Revenge standards, their "sound" wasn't half-bad. Their presence on stage was an abomination, a travesty that culminated in a staged pillow fight between the girls that wound up trashing the stage - the pillows were stuffed with miniature marshmallows.

Nixon's Revenge became punk rock legends based on that one show and were invited to headline a backyard party hosted by KSAK DJ B. David Hollenbeck. This time Nixon's Revenge had time to prepare and Mr. P laid out an ambitious game plan - a gig with African chants, staged slam dunks and loads of controversy. By this time, Darlene and Donna were full-fledged members of the group, contributing song material and inviting many of their own Mt. Sac poetry class friends, including MJ Stevens, Donna's ex-husband, as well as her current husband, guitarist Terry Churchman.

More Gorillas were included. Nixon's Revenge's song list went heavy on shock - Mr. P alone brought out several lamentably titled songs in addition to the song that more than any other pointed the way to Desperation Squad - "Hispanics on TV".

On Easter Sunday 1980, Mr. P was watching late night TV

and chanced upon one of those Public Service programs required at the time by the FCC. This program consisted of Hispanic Americans venting much rage at U.S. policy. It was heated, heavy stuff, extremely important to the participant, ranting at Jimmy Carter and loudly offering solutions to improve their community - and completely buried by the network in a time slot where no one would watch. "Hispanics On T.V." was born. It was a dance song with Temptations-inspired refrains of "Get down! Get on down!" It needed strong guitar to keep the beat. Alan suggested a 16-year old kid taking lessons at the Guitar Store, Jeff Hayes. Hayes came in, found a lick, Alan gladly hopped on the drums, Peterson on bass, and Mr. P on vocals and wretched harmonica, and Nixon's Revenge had their first "hit."

The San Dimas backyard party gig undid everything the Mt. Sac gig had fomented - a punk rock band was supposed to churn out fast and simple songs you slammed to, not a conceptual mishmash of badly played comedy routines. The heavily KSAK crowd, hammered after a full day of drinking, could not handle it. It was close to a full hour before "Hispanics On T.V." was played, the only song remotely close to a crowd pleaser. All the rest fell flat, including "Humphreys Triple" and Brian's "We Ain't Getting No Pussy Tonight". Yet Nixon's Revenge had found an audience of new admirers - Darlene and Donna's quirky friends. And they had found a permanent guitar player - Jeff Hayes would remain in the group and play a major role.

Nixon's Revenge staked out its own increasingly polarizing terrain, accentuated by strict artistic philosophies, such as playing all-new material every show and never practicing until the night before a gig. Nixon's Revenge shows were chaotic and exasperating for both band and audience alike, although their dada-esque approach brought them much closer to the punk ideal of anarchy than most of the other punk bands of the day.

Spudz, the opening band at the San Dimas backyard party, contacted **Mr. P to be the lead singer of the newly renamed Bad Attitude**, which was scheduled to play a show at the Pomona Skateland. Mr. P was ecstatic and worked with Gene "Uncle Remus" Richau, his brother Dave and guitarist Robbo DeVille to hammer together a typically aggressive punk rock set, with a couple of Sex Pistols covers and two Mr. P originals.

Opening the show was the debut performance of The Dull, a band that featured Sirdar Dizaye on bass and Harold Clements on guitar. The Dull would go on to establish itself as one of Pomona's main punk bands, as well as a key ally of both Nixon's Revenge and Desperation Squad. Bob Jones, Alan Waddington and Ian Carlson all performed with The Dull at various times and Robbo DeVille would eventually join The Dull himself.

Spudz opened for Nixons Revenge, then offered lead singer slot to Mr. P.

Though Bad Attitude was a prototypical punk band, Mr. P demonstrated immediately he was not the typical punk lead singer—dancing spastically, bringing out props and, to the disgust of all, incorporating food into the act. The Skateland crowd revolted, yanking the chain-link fence barrier out of the ground and began throwing bottles and trash at Mr. P, who finished the gig with a severe cut on his hand. Still, he considered the show a success and was eager to introduce new material for the next show. Bad Attitude had different ideas and fired Mr. P after one gig for not being "punk" enough.

A bit stung by the dismissal, Mr. P was determined to get his own group together and found an eager partner in Hayes. Fellow Diamond Bar buddies Brian

Hudson on drums and Tim Allyn on bass were recruited to form The Blortemus, an incomprehensible name derived from the twisted language devised by Hudson and his older brother Bob.

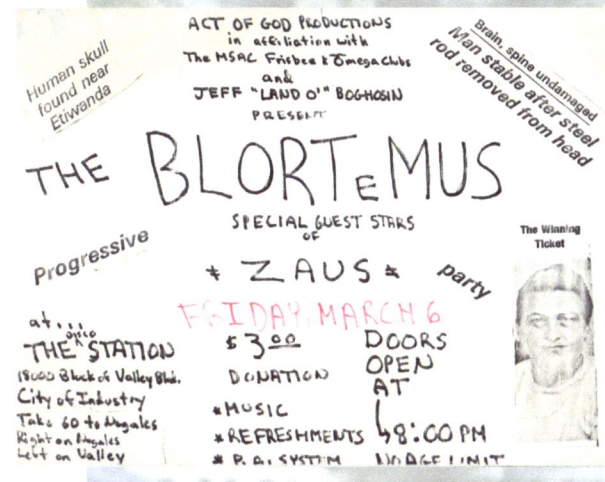

Hayes and Hudson both became prolific writers

within the group and by the end of 1980 the band had a huge pool of songs to choose from, including "Please Don't Eat My Food" and "Infatuated" by Hayes and "D.S. Special" and "You're A Fake" by Hudson. There were even contributions from outside the band, like Jeff Spizser's "What's A Half-Life?" and a couple Alan Waddington Nixon's Revenge compositions, "Reenie's A Tease" and "Volleyball Distractions (Your Girlfriend's Ugly)", songs that would eventually become classics for Desperation Squad. Oddly, Mr. P's song production was rather weak during this period. He wrote only one new song for The Blortemus, but it was pivotal: "Amity (A Song About Love)."

Lyrically, "Amity" was a bit brutal, which is why it never advanced beyond The Blortemus.

> Mr. P: "Up to this point, I wrote either irreverent songs like 'Food' and 'Hispanics On T.V.' or somewhat twisted lonelyheart songs like "Angel Of Mercy" or "I Can't Find No One (Who Wants To Be My Girlfriend)". I was the strikeout king with girls, couldn't even get a date and I kept trying to get to my 'true feelings', which was not working. 'Amity' was completely different. She was Hayes' girlfriend and their relationship was one of constant screaming, yelling and fighting. One day I just got inspired and wrote down all his complaints in song form. It was the first time I acted as an independent observer of love, not someone ravaged by its effects. It clicked. I found my voice. Without 'Amity' there's no 'That Thing' or 'Mr. Fireworks' or 'Serious Love' or 'Breaking Nobody's Heart'. Once I realized I could channel my moods, make it humorous and put some decent hooks on it, it changed the whole way I approached songwriting, to this day."

AMITY:
(a song about love)

I don't ever want to see you again
Amity, Amity
The way you're playing I'll never win
Amity, Amity
Your constant bitching is bad for my health
You arbitrarily put me on the shelf
Why don't you just go fuck yourself
Amity

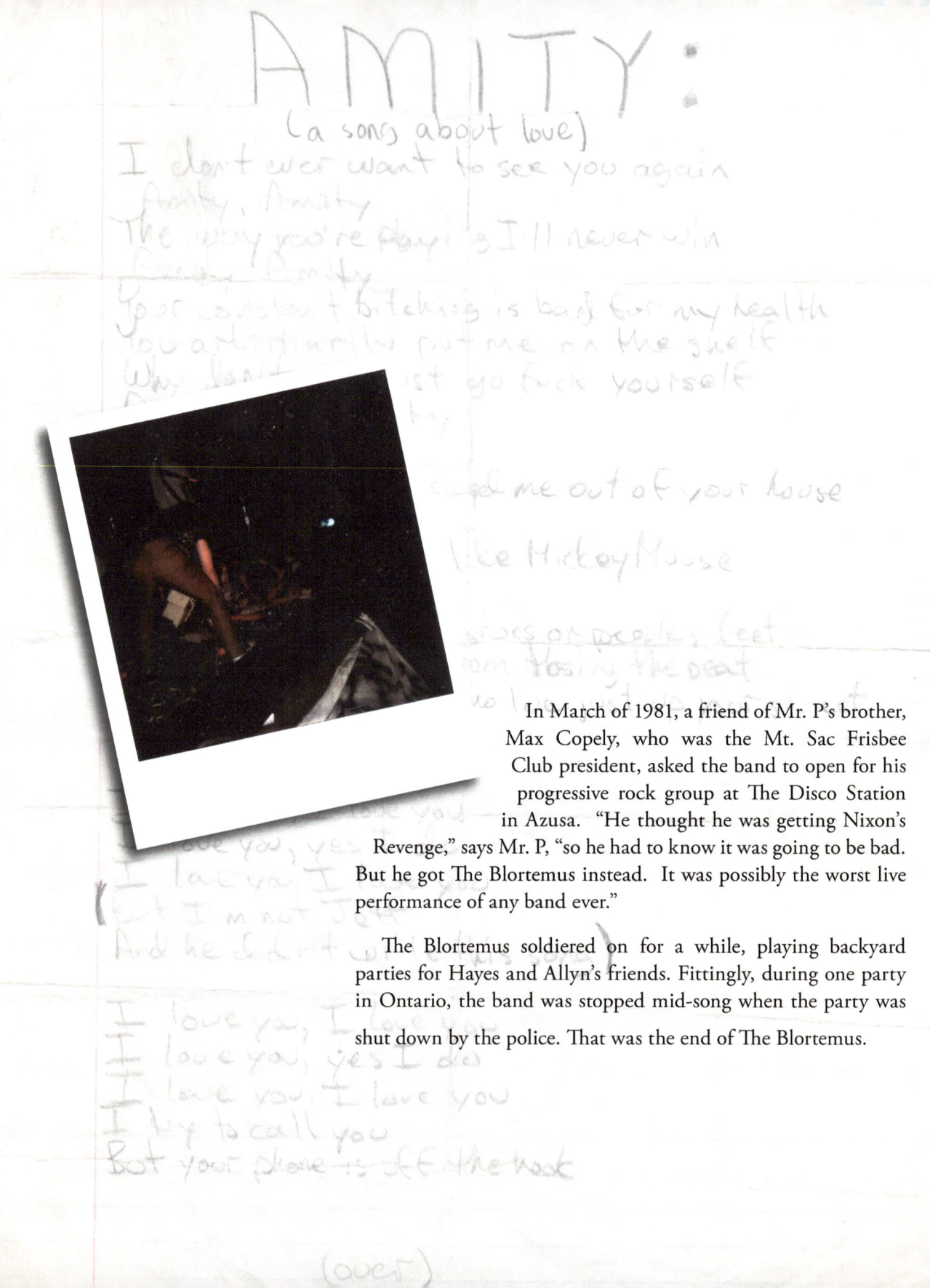

...ed me out of your house
...
... like Mickey Mouse
...
...shoes on people's feet
...from losing the beat
...

I love you, I love you
I love you, yes I do
I love you, I love you
But I'm not Joe
And he didn't ...

I love you, I love you
I love you, yes I do
I love you, I love you
I try to call you
But your phone is off the hook

(over)

In March of 1981, a friend of Mr. P's brother, Max Copely, who was the Mt. Sac Frisbee Club president, asked the band to open for his progressive rock group at The Disco Station in Azusa. "He thought he was getting Nixon's Revenge," says Mr. P, "so he had to know it was going to be bad. But he got The Blortemus instead. It was possibly the worst live performance of any band ever."

The Blortemus soldiered on for a while, playing backyard parties for Hayes and Allyn's friends. Fittingly, during one party in Ontario, the band was stopped mid-song when the party was shut down by the police. That was the end of The Blortemus.

Hoppy Price was an aerospace engineer at JPL and friend of Donna and Terry Churchman. **Hoppy had a small recording studio at his home in La Cañada.** The subsequent Nixon's Revenge sessions became the only true lasting legacy of the band with influence that would eventually create an entire separate music scene of its own.

The first session was dominated by Alan/Mr. P/Hayes and included the "hits" "Hispanics on TV" and "Good Mood" as well as "Bad Girl" written by Darlene's boyfriend Brad McCown and sung by Mr. P. The second session was looser and featured more contributors. Dave Carpenter, who along with older brother Paul hosted Gorilla body-surfing parties at their parents Balboa Beach house, sang and played on Brian W's "The Richardson Family" as well as his own composition "Brooks Takes Charge", which was sung with true punk rock bravado by Brad McCown.

There was no attempt to "shop" the recordings or issue any vinyl, but the recordings were passed among the bands seemingly never to see the light of day again.

Mr. P's brother John lived at a hippie crash pad called the Gordon House with long-time friend Chuck Hackett. Over the years many depraved parties, some with Stratus, were thrown there. In Feb. of 1980, Mr. P went to a cast party for the Mt. Sac play "One Flew Over the Cuckoo's Nest" in which John had a featured role. At the party Mr. P met Larry Wilmore, then attending Cal Poly Pomona and involved in the Mt. Sac Drama Dept. Mr. P also met Martin Kauper, with whom he would enter into a lifelong creative relationship. In the fall, Mr. P would be cast in "A Flea In Her Ear" with John, Wilmore and Kauper. On opening night, a lamentable mishap caused Kauper to miss an entrance, leading to the inspiration for a Kauper-produced Super-8 movie "The 39 Saps" in which Mr. P had a small role. It was the first of many creative collaborations between the two. Despite Mr. P's occasional forays into rock performance, he

The cast of "A Flea in Her Ear": Daniel Gutierrez, Marlene Wiscovitch, Mr. P, Larry Wilmore, Teena Nickolas, and Dave Wilson

was still greatly focused on a career in radio. By the fall of 1981, he had secured a regular evening shift. One night Kauper approached him with a radio play he had written and Mr. P agreed to a one-time only live radio theater broadcast. For the next year and a half on Monday nights The "P" Shufflers performed original scripts written primarily by Kauper, Mr. P and Raymond Schaefer.

In Spring 1982 the two embarked on an epic production that would take an entire year to complete. The result, "Shuffling Around The Dial", an homage to the Firesign Theater, debuted at the 1983 Drama Dept. banquet. Mr. P played Raymond Booth, Private Sleuth, who spent the entire movie chasing TV bad guys The Obnoxious Bros across multiple channels in an attempt to "save" TV. Several hilarious scenes from the two-reel 40-minute film proved a big hit when shown at a "Super-8 Night" screening at Al's Bar in Los Angeles later that year. Two in particular stood out. "Familiar Affair" - where a psychotic Mr. French has just inexplicably butchered Uncle Bill and then turns his anger to Buffy and Jodie. Stealing the show was Alan and Brian Hudson as the Obnoxious Brothers, yarring and harring their way into the Cal Arts-heavy crowd who, after having spent the night watching their own arty films, were quite astonished by these outsider's irreverence and gal.

Nixon's Revenge played the majority of their gigs in 1980

and 1981, including a show at a community festival at the Chino Fairgrounds. Mr. P's passion for messy props began here with the song, "Food". Somewhat incredibly, the band returned to Mt. Sac for a show the day after Ronald Reagan was elected president. That gig showed the debut of Alan's tribute to their favorite Diamond Bar party chick, "Reenie's A Tease", and Mr. P's "Isla Vista", written after several trips to UC Santa Barbara to visit Rob Stahl and his brother Dave. At a backyard for Michael Bluestein, Alan unleashed "Volleyball Distractions" with its genius chorus, "Your girlfriend's ugly, MOTHERFUCKER!!" To Mr. P's chagrin, two shows were booked during his run in "A Flea In Her Ear".

In 1981, Darlene and Donna introduced Nixon's Revenge to **Art DiLion, who had just acquired a space way down on the eastern edge of the Pomona Mall on 2nd Street, named simply Arts Building.** At one time or another every band or artist in the Pomona punk rock underground funneled through Arts Bldg., thanks to Art's all-inclusive hands-off booking policy. It was where Rozz Williams was photographed by Edward Colver at his solo show, which included young drummer Mary Torregrossa.

Jill Emery, newly graduated from Ganesha High School, found immediate refuge at Arts, with her friend Myrna Aviles. After the Iggy Pop concert years before, Emery cropped her hair and picked up a bass. She became perhaps Pomona's first true punk rocker, and founded many seminal bands of the day, including Disfigured Faces, Superheroines and The Decadent.

Art DiLion was particularly fond of Nixon's Revenge, and was in fact another of the strand of the Darlene/Donna Mt. Sac network of friends and artists. This network included a brilliant young painter, Robert Jones, who also happened to play an extraordinary upside down left handed guitar. Along with MJ Stevens, another experimental guitarist, they formed

the Blue Mysterioso and played not only Arts Building but also G5, which is where Mr. P first encountered the estimable Mr. Jones.

Arts Building became Nixon's Revenge's home base, since no one else would book them - except, oddly, Mt. Sac, which never seemed to figure out booking Nixon's Revenge was always a disaster. A higher profile gig with Moslem Birth was cancelled when punks set fire to the dumpster outside Arts.

A Nixon's Revenge gig was booked for the Unitarian Church in Montclair. Before the show Mr. P went to Alan with the lyrics to a new song that needed structure. "That thing, that crazy little thing you do to me". The two cobbled together an arrangement for that show. "That Thing" showed potential and so intrigued Alan that he willingly broke a cardinal Nixon's Revenge rule - he brought the song back to play the next gig at Mt. Sac, this time with Rod Curtis on bass and Hayes on guitar. Mr. P and Alan both came to a stunning conclusion - "That Thing" was a hit.

After a spectacular run, Stratus petered out around the end of 1982, due to various band tensions and disagreements over new material, which was never really Stratus' strong suit. They were a party band and the party scene was changing. Time to move on.

Alan Waddington had no shortage of work. A disciple of iconic jazz drummer Les DeMerle, (Alan and Mr. P hung out at DeMerle's club The Cellar in Los Angeles all the time). Alan always had two or three or more gigs going at the same time.

In 1983 he met Ray Woodbury, who played guitar for a local band called The Escorts, which featured a dynamic young singer named Rebecca Hamm. The Escorts played at a local dance club in Pomona where Mr. P and fellow Stratus/Diamond Bar friend Pat Lott used to go. Waddington also teamed up with Curtis and Hayes to form The Thunderbirds, a party band. The Thunderbirds played mostly covers, but was much looser than Stratus, to the point of bringing up Mr. P to guest-sing on "That Thing". Eager to erase a string of dismal gigs with Nixon's Revenge and The Blortemus, Mr. P was pumped and ready. The power grooves provided by Waddington, Curtis and Hayes set the table; all Mr. P had to do was nail it. "That Thing" was a big fat crowd-pleasing hit, brought to life in a big way by Hayes' inspired guitar.

Tues., July 30 — *Bedrock, Dave Gage, Automatics.* Downstairs: *The Vanguards, Desperation Squad, The Escorts.*
Wed., July 31 — *611 and S.O.S, Telefones, The Odd.* Downstairs: *Rising Sun, The Model.*

In the official program for "Shuffling Around The Dial", a send-up of TV Guide (called the "TV Died") dated May 1983, the listing for a show called "Rock Town" showed three names: "Nixon's Revenge" (whose footage of "The Star Spangled Banner" didn't make the final cut), "J. Hayes and the Thunderbirds", and a band that existed only in Mr. P's head - "Desperation Squad".

Dave Carpenter, who had played and recorded with Nixon's Revenge, shared the recordings with his friends from Claremont High - Mark Givens, Joel Huschle, and Tim Kirk. The psychotically happy "Good Mood" by Alan, one of the highlights of the San Dimas gig, fit right in with what Carpenter and Kirk were doing in their band The Love Bunnies, and they performed "Good Mood" at a large show at Claremont High opening for the legendary Posh Boy recording artists The Stepmothers, featuring Steve Jones and Jay Lansford, (future bandmates of Alan Waddington in The Unforgiven). On the same bill was Red Brigade, a band

37

fronted by Kurt Ross, who the D-Squad would cross paths with time and again over the coming years.

The 82-83 school year was crazy busy, with a weekly "P" Theater, shooting the movie, performing Children's Theatre (which Waddington was also involved) and both Kauper and Mr. P were directing plays for the MSAC Player's Club. Mr. P was also spending a lot of time at KROQ, where some of his "P" Theater scripts made the rounds. Mr. P spent a lot of time in the production room with DJ John Logic and some fringe writers who produced occasional comedy spots.

For Mr. P, the future was looking bright

— he was creatively stable, he was fulfilling his dream of being a disc jockey and a writer and performer, and he was dabbling in a little rock-starring on the side. He embraced the new development as far as it went but clearly radio was the pony to bet on; he'd spent five years at it and it was paying off. Mr. P wrote a new song, "Mr. Fireworks", another refreshingly upbeat number with the chorus, "Who's gonna be Mr. Fireworks tonight?/I'm gonna be Mr. Fireworks tonight!!"

Bob Jones booked Nixon's Revenge a gig at Shamus O'Brien's in El Monte, where Jones played with Nixon's Revenge for the first time, along with 13-year-old Ian Carlson, a drum student of Alan's who lived around the corner from Hayes in Diamond Bar. Mr. P sang "Mr. Fireworks" and "Can't Go In Crowds", his two strongest rockers in ages.

Things were indeed looking bright. But soon, it was all going to change.

For the fall semester at MSAC, Kauper decided to direct "Play It Again, Sam" by Woody Allen. Mr. P drove out to Samuel French in Hollywood to pick a play of his own and walked out with "Hooters", a risque coming of age comedy by Ted Tally. "Hooters" did quite well, with nice advertising posters and a photo spread in the Pomona Progress Bulletin, taken by staff photographer Walt Weis.

"P" Theater had entered its second year with a barrel full of recurring characters, with silly names like Clancy Humphunger and Capt. Erwin, which Martin and Mr. P would weave in and out of episodes and the more frequent extra bits they were throwing in. For "P" Theater, it was top-dollar stuff. For KSAK management it was just annoying.

In August 1983 "P" Theater staged its most elaborate production ever - "Gorilla Game of the Week" - where they used practically the entire radio program to broadcast a fake baseball game between the Gorillas and their arch-rivals the Mandingos from the South End of Diamond Bar, rankling the feathers of KSAK management even further.

Mr. P had hit a similar dead end at KROQ. Up to this point, radio was Mr. P's life, the reason he was Mr. P. And now he was at a crossroads.

Story by JOSEPH H. FIRMAN
PB Entertainment Editor
Photos by WALT WEIS
PB photographer

"Hooters" director Kevin Ausmus, center, gives some pointers to Julie Segovia (Cheryl) and Steve Arnold (Clint). The comedy is set for April 15 and 16 at 8 p.m.

In early 1983, Mr. P, Alan, Jeff and Rod Curtis drove out to Eric Sklar's studio to record "That Thing". It was a watershed moment, the first time that Mr. P had funded a recording project on his own. It wasn't a Thunderbirds or a Nixon's Revenge song, it was something different, an entirely new creation. The gears were churning.

In October, Mr. P got cast in a community theater production of "Ten Little Indians" at the Gallery Theatre in Ontario where he played Marston, the ill-fated young hipster, and had a nice choking scene in the 1st Act. One night after a show he drove to Diamond Bar for a Halloween party featuring the Thunderbirds - unfortunately missing the opening band Cosmic Hoss, with Ian Carlson, singer/guitarist Jerry O'Sullivan and bassist Dan Irving.

In March 1984 Mr. P accepted a small role in "Arsenic and Old Lace", appearing only a little at the beginning and end. One night he left the premises to drive to a Lorbeer Jr. High dance where The Thunderbirds were playing. In his stage duds and makeup, Mr. P came up to sing "That Thing" for the 8th graders, including the Cosmic Hoss kids, and drove back to finish his play.

He was gone from radio, from Mt. Sac, and was unemployed. He needed a creative outlet that would define him.

He was living at G5 and more than a little bit lonely since ditching radio and everything that had kept him somewhat planted in reality. One night, the phone rang with an invitation to dinner with Keith Misumi and some of his friends. Mr. P brightened considerably and went to take a shower to get ready.

In the time it took for Mr. P to take a shower, find a pencil and paper, Desperation Squad was officially born. Where "Humphrey's Triple" had pointed the way; "Hispanics On T.V." had established a standard; "That Thing" provided the impetus and "Mr. Fireworks" the positive attitude, bottom line they were all Nixon's Revenge songs.

"I walk into the room and
There's a kind of a hush
You all are oh so envious
You want to be me if you could
Cuz I'm - looking good!"

"Looking Good" was the first bonafide Desperation Squad song. Mr. P had been rolling the name around in his head for a couple of years, a bold name that stood out in an era of synth-rock, post-punk and roots rockers. Desperation Squad was to be avant-garde pop that was crazy and funny, Nixon's Revenge with a decent P.A. and a permanent set list.

That was the goal. In reality, the band barely existed beyond Mr. P, Alan, and Hayes. Waddington was clearly the key player. Without his experience and ability to bring together disparate musicians, D-Squad would likely suffer the same fate as The Blortemus. Waddington's enthusiasm for the project put a stamp of legitimacy on Desperation Squad but to be Desperation Squad, there needed to be more, something no one was expecting.

When Alan arranged for "Looking Good" to be recorded at Cal State Fullerton, Mr. P knew the song would

ROBERT JONES
BACCHUS 43" × 43"

Bob Jones was already an established artist when D-Squad made its debut

need some extra oomph. He had long been fascinated by Bob Jones' guitar work. Jones was asleep on his couch when Mr. P called.

Arriving at the studio, Jones met Hayes for the first time. The basic tracks were laid with Alan on drums and Hayes on bass and rhythm guitar. Jones was then given his own track to solo over. Jones' indescribable heavily Velvet Underground-influenced riffs were like nothing anybody had heard, least of all Hayes, who studied classically trained guitarists like Steve Howe of Yes and technically prescient guitarists like Frank Zappa. Hayes' jaw dropped and he wasn't quite sure he wanted to share the stage with someone who was just making it up as he went along. Yet, **the team of Hayes/Jones became the lynchpin of D-Squad's sound**, and despite the polar opposite approaches on guitar, Jeff and Bob became fast friends.

But who would play bass? Rod Curtis had no interest. Paul Peterson had been out of the loop for quite some time and Tim Allyn was just finishing up a two-year stint in the Marines. Alan had been working for the Citrus College Music Department and dipped into the talent pool and brought forth Laura Kovach of Covina.

Laura was 18 years old, but looked like she was 13, almost ridiculously cute and enthusiastic. Now, the band with the weird name and oddball songs looked exactly like it sounded - unorthodox yet appealing; underground but somehow mainstream, sort of. Five players who looked like they should be in five separate bands.

Desperation Squad's debut gig on the back of a pick-up truck in the Sav-On parking lot occurred on May 19, 1984. The line-up: Mr. P, Alan, Laura, Jeff, and Bob, with Ian providing a bit of Nixon's Revenge on trumpet. There were no power outages, no enraged track coaches, no

SAV-ON

bottles thrown, no cops called. Ray Woodbury was there, helping out with the sound, Dave Carpenter and Joel Huschle from Wckr Spgt were there, and a couple dozen Diamond Bar friends came to show support.

It wasn't great. It didn't suck. In fact, the complete lack of controversy made the show fairly innocuous. No one in attendance, not even the band, felt as if an earth-shattering event had taken place. Humphrey's Triple, Hispanics On TV, That Thing, Looking Good, Mr. Fireworks, The Club, Reenie's A Tease, Night of the Living Dead, Your Girlfriends Ugly and Hang On Sloopy made up the set.

Afterwards, everyone retired to nearby G5 for beers, weed and congratulatory high fives. If you had asked anyone what was next for the band, the answer would have been unanimously "I don't know".

Soon enough, fate would decide Desperation Squad's next move.

PVA

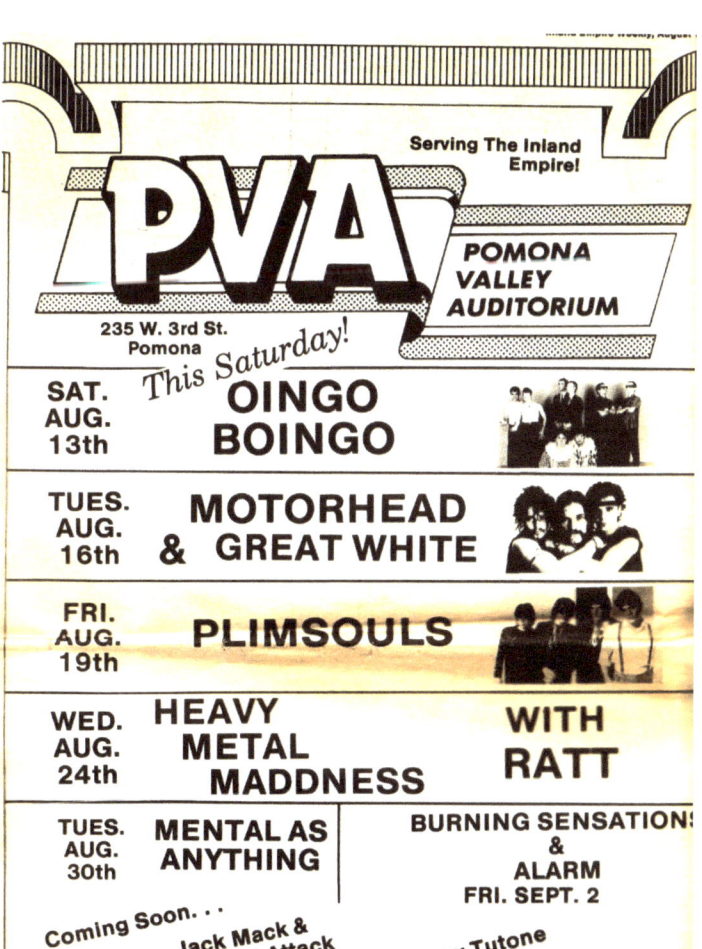

In August of 1983 the Pomona Valley Auditorium, the PVA, opened amid great fanfare, bringing an unconventional mix of punk rock, heavy metal and new wave to the area for the first time. Located in the forever shuttered United Artists movie theater, the PVA hit the ground running, their debut night featuring the immensely popular Oingo Boingo, with an unknown group opening for them, raising considerable hackles among the crowd. That band was the Red Hot Chili Peppers, making the first of several appearances at the PVA.

Despite the impressive roster of bands that gigged there - The Ramones, R.E.M., Cheap Trick, Loudness among them -

mismanagement and lousy marketing plagued the PVA from the beginning. It didn't help that although they had a license to sell beer, you could only drink it in the lobby, not on the floor. Still, the PVA played a very important role in the development of Desperation Squad, whose first pivotal gigs and publicity came via the music venue.

ROCK WARS

If Desperation Squad's first show was a triumph simply for the fact it was completed without incident, their next show neatly encapsulated the delightful polarization the band would provide to audiences over the next 30 years, and made good a general observation Mr. P had made, "The worst thing for a band is for people to have no opinion of them." The "Rock Wars" show clearly delineated that there was no middle ground with the Squad, you either loved them or hated them. Two guitar players, one tall and lanky, wearing short shorts, the other swarthy and stout playing incomprehensible upside down feedback, a chick bass player

Mr. P relaxes before the big show

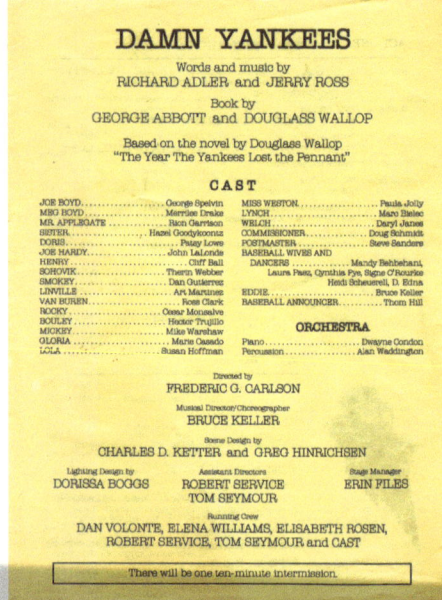

who looked 15 years old, an out of control recently discharged Marine prancing around menacingly, an unruffled drummer calmly keeping the chaos in check, and a front man who scream-sang lyrics about suburban swim clubs, cockteasing babes and third string baseball players while bopping spastically to the rhythm.

"Rock Wars" was the brainchild of Max Copley, the band's old buddy from Mt. Sac, who was staging a local battle of the bands with a grand prize of $700 and 10 hours of recording time at the Music Store in Walnut, where Copley worked. At first Mr. P (along with brother John) was recruited as a judge, meting out harsh assessments of the very same "ordinary" metal/glam bands he loathed. Inquiring about a possible D-Squad gig, Copley informed Mr. P that participating bands paid $450 upfront and hustled pre-sale tickets, an early

Bob and Alan backstage (w/Harold Clements from the Dull)

"pay-to-play" format Mr. P knew the band couldn't pull off. Then, two days later, Mr. P received an impassioned phone call from Copley. One of the other bands had dropped out and they needed a replacement ASAP, pre-sale requirements overlooked.

Once offered the slot, Mr. P had to determine if the band could, in fact, play it. One huge obstacle was that Alan Waddington was already committed to performing in the musical Damn Yankees at Citrus College. Mr. P went to a "Rock Wars" band meeting, where the night's lineup would be determined through a random draw. Mr. P immediately volunteered for the final slot, hoping that no one else wanted it. The ploy worked, resolving scheduling conflicts and getting Desperation Squad onto the bill. Not only was D-Squad competing for a chance at the grand prize, they weren't paying any upfront money and the winner would be announced only after the crowd had to sit through their set!

EXHIBIT A

ROCK WARS INFO SHEET

The "ROCK WARS" is designed to showcase local talent and give local bands the chance to gain exposure as well as the chance of winning an album project. Below are the rules and procedures for this event.

Each band will be provided with 150 (One hundred fifty) tickets. (Each band will be limited to 150 pre-sale tickets.) The price printed on the tickets is $6.00. It is recommended that the bands sell advance tickets at $1.00 discount. When the band sells all 150 tickets at $5.00 each, they will make a profit of $300.00. If the band chooses to sell the tickets at full face value, their profit margin will be greater and they will reach breakeven on the $450.00 investment earlier.

Sequence of performance of bands will be determined by a random drawing at a meeting held at P.V.A. on the Thursday evening, at 8 P.M., prior to the performance. Band members from each band should plan to attend this meeting. Other important information such as house rules, introduction of crew heads, dressing room facilities, etc., will be discussed.

Each band will be permitted to admit only six crew members. There will be no other guest passes or additional crew member passes available.

- continued -

KA
(Initial here)

"Rock Wars" was one of the first instances of "pay to play", where bands were coerced to put up large chunks of cash to secure a gig, then hustle to sell tickets to their friends, a practice that became commonplace throughout the 80s and beyond.

ROCK WARS

Laura and Jeff all tuned up and ready to go.

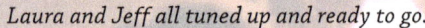

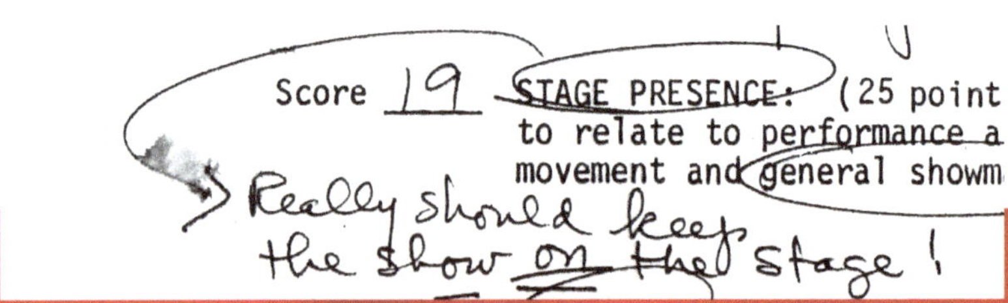

Score 19 STAGE PRESENCE: (25 point
to relate to performance a
movement and general showm
Really should keep
the show ~~on the~~ stage!

Bob Jones rocks it while chaos reigns.

Among the other bands at "Rock Wars" was The Dash, featuring 14 year old Jon Crawford on drums and Sean Sullivan on guitar. From South Diamond Bar, their paths would cross with D-Squad many times over the years.

Shortly after the Sav-On parking lot show, Tim Allyn had been discharged from the Marines. Too late to be the D-Squad bass player, Mr. P thought he could be of use to the band in some capacity so he invited Allyn to join the band as "dancer/percussionist". The result: Tim Allyn whipped around the stage like a leopard-robed tornado, drawing flak and derisive taunts from the crowd. 20 minutes into the show, during "Humphrey's Triple", he went flying off the stage and into the audience and started a brawl. The band never missed a beat. Mr. P held up a poster of Reggie Jackson, screamed "Reggie!" and D-Squad managed to complete their set in the required 30 minute set duration requirement (points were deducted for going three minutes over; Waddington timed the show on his watch, the band clocking in at 32:45!).

Not only was the band *not* disqualified but, incredibly, they had easily won over the judges, several of whom fairly gushed their approval. One judge noted "Best group all night!" "Great songs, Reggie!" "Very stimulating performance!" and compared Mr. P to David Letterman, while giving the Squad 95 out of 100 points! They scored 81 on another ballot, and another, while awarding them an average 73 (dismissing their Tonality, which he noted was "not a requirement of your particular format"), thanked the band for being so fun and "not taking yourselves so seriously". Even the one

Desperation Squad's performance exceeded all reasonable expectations, causing one "music industry" judge, F. Atencio, to gush effusively in his praise, awarding the band 95 points out of a possible 100, not to mention commentary that bordered on fanatical.

judge who hated the band, giving them a 41 total, summed up the experience like this (scrawled almost illegibly on the back of the ballot): "This world is not ready for two Mick Jagger".

Two gigs into his rock career and Mr. P was already being compared to Mick Jagger!

A rumor circulated that the Squad had the best overall scores but in the end, cries of "fix" were rampant as Mr. P's brother, John, had remained on the judges panel. John, by the way, gave the Squad a score of 79. While this deep-sixed the band's chances of moving on to the finals, it's hard to imagine an encore performance topping this show.

A month later, a group featuring Ian Carlson and Jerry O'Sullivan - Grand Prix (pronounced 'pricks') - made their own appearance at "Rock Wars", also with Waddington on drums and The Unforgiven's Steve Jones on guitar.

The Chili Peppers popularity didn't prevent a local poster company from botching their name!

Since their rambunctious debut at the PVA in August of 1983, the Red Hot Chili Peppers had ascended quickly, signing a big record deal within months and establishing themselves as one of the biggest drawing bands in Los Angeles.

Concert Organizer Pat Bacich (who had met Mr. P years earlier at the Galaxy West in San Dimas) scored his biggest gig to date, a phenomenal double bill with the Chili Peppers and Agent Orange at the PVA. With two spots open for local bands, Bacich offered

DESPERATION SQUAD

"A SLAM-BANG FUN FEST..."
"FUNNY, EXQUISITELY PERFORMED..."
"IT'S A DAZZLER!"
"SHIVERINGLY MEMORABLE"

P.V.A. Pomona
35 W. 3rd
SAT 25 JAN.

---

single line."

Power Tool looked like a Cecil B. DeMille production, with a fleet of limos outside and a cast of thousands glamorously jamming the lobby and draped up the sweeping steps to a Union Station-sized ballroom seething with the Saturday-night dance-till-you-drop marathon party crowd. Elegant **Europa** (decked out in dazzlingly beaded harem garb) and the buxom **Jane Cantillon** combined their feminine wiles to entertain the downstairs crowd after **Lawndale** had rattled the marble halls with their surfy din. Among those who stopped by to check out **Matt Dike**'s cool cuts were **George Clinton** (fresh from the Chili Peppers/Desperation Squad gig in Pomona), **Fab Five Freddie** and screenwriter-to-Prince **Becky Johnston**, **Michael Korey** (Radwaste), **Norwood** (Fishbone), **Bob Forrest**, **Jellybean Benitez** with Steve (Warners) **Tipp**, and Mr. and Mrs. **Carlos Guitarlos**.

What me worry? Bluesy Robert Cray displays bad influences at Lingerie. *Reynaldo Rivera*

them up to The Flamethrowers and Desperation Squad. Mr. P had met L.A. Weekly gossip writer Shelly da Cunha several months earlier and made an effort to keep the band on her radar. Gigging with the Chili Peppers proved irresistible for da Cunha, who name-dropped the D-Squad in her LA Dee Dah column, cleverly working them into an item about Freaky Styley producer George Clinton.

According to the L.A. Weekly, George Clinton was among the audience members at PVA show.

In one of the most bizarre shows the band would ever play, Desperation Squad returned to the PVA for the third and final time as the opening act on a dream bill of pioneering punk band 'X' and, again, the Red Hot Chili Peppers. Both headliners were going through transition periods. 'X' was pursuing a more mainstream pop-metal sound, having replaced Billy Zoom with Blasters and Knitters guitarist Dave Alvin. The Chili Peppers were at the tail end of their long arduous tour for Freaky Styley. They had just fired drummer Cliff Martinez a few weeks earlier and replaced him with founding member Jack Irons, meaning that the PVA show was the first LA area show with the original Chili Peppers lineup since 1983. D-Squad's inclusion on the bill was an amazing coup, but came close to not happening thanks to the show's promoter being less than forthcoming about many facets of the production, according to Mr. P.

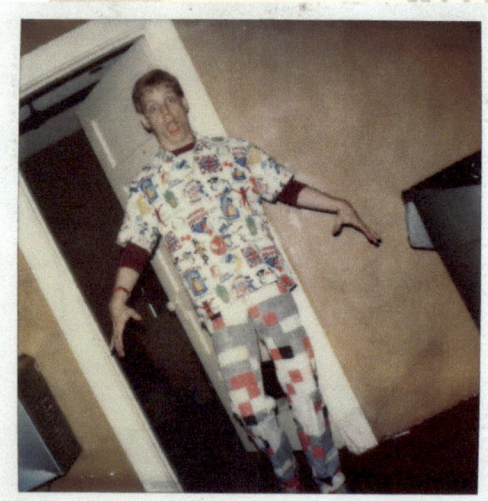

"Pat Bacich had recommended us for the show after another band dropped out maybe two weeks before. But the promoter at the PVA was an idiot. He couldn't make up his mind whether to put us on the show or not and suddenly it was, like, one day before the show and we still didn't know. We couldn't tell anybody because we didn't want to look like total jerks if we didn't play the gig. So I started calling around. I called X's people. I called the Chili Pepper's people. Their reaction was bizarre, like they had no idea what was going on either. I thought, 'How the hell do you not know how your band is playing a show in the next night?' This is how: It was a secret. The Chili Peppers had

some hokey rule they couldn't open for anyone, not even a band like 'X'. Later that evening I get a call, 'Yeah you're on the gig' and then 15 minutes later the guy calls back and is screaming at me, 'What the hell did you do? We almost had to cancel the whole fucking gig!' I'm not sure why he didn't shit-can us right there but he didn't. When I showed up at the PVA though, every single person there connected to the show was pissed as shit at me for fucking everything up. Nice, classy people. Even with all that, the show was great. People were lined up around the block to get in and we played in front of a sellout crowd for the first time. Some of our friends were there and they totally freaked out when they saw us come on stage. And everyone was blown away by us. The other bands were fired up too. I heard about Anthony Kiedis going around saying, 'They got a song called Great Big Boogers In Your Nose!" And the word is that both Exene and John Doe came up from the backstage to watch us and that Doe left to get his smokes and raced back so he wouldn't miss any of the show. It was all pretty thrilling."

57

L to R: Jeff Hayes, Laura Kovach, Mr. P, Ian Carlson, Bob Jones. The same lineup would play the Warped Tour 17 years later.

Desperation Squad didn't have to wait too long to follow up on their 1984 "Rock Wars" PVA triumph. Shortly after the gig they were contacted again by Bacich to play a show at a shuttered steakhouse located on Route 66 in Azusa called **Oscar's Cornhusker.** It was the first of several unlikely settings Bacich converted into showcases for a newly burgeoning San Gabriel Valley music scene. For the next year or so Oscars hosted most of the bands commonly associated with D-Squad at that time:

John Henry Jones, Just Jones, Johnny Hickman of the Unforgiven get first glimpse of D-Squad

The Unforgiven, The Dull, Silver Chalice, Psych 201 and the bands who comprised the rest of the bill that night - The Flamethrowers and the Stan West Band.

The Flamethrowers were led by singer Kurt Ross, who had previously fronted Red Brigade, Kent State and the Wild Ones, and Steve Alba, the legendary skateboarder, who Mr. P had met in 1980 when he worked at Music Plus in Pomona. Stan West was a respected blues guitarist who seemingly had given music lessons to every up and coming punk rocker in town.

The Oscar's show was significant in many ways. It came amid a flurry of activity outside the band. Alan Wadddington was busy preparing for the debut performance of The Unforgiven, which was only a week away. Bob Jones had just staged a solo art show at Claremont Graduate University.

59

OSCAR'S CORNHUSKER

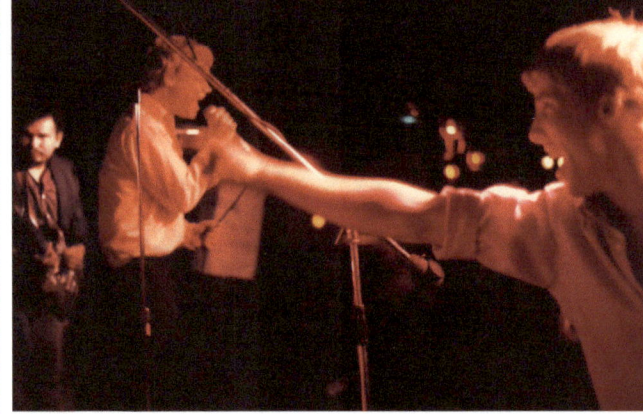

Bob, Mr. P and Jeff Spiszer

Mr. P had landed the lead role in another community play, "The Good Doctor" being staged at St. Paul's Church in Pomona. Also, the '84 Olympics had just blown through Los Angeles, with Mr. P and Waddington attending the Brazil-Italy basketball game at the Forum (and running into a befuddled USA coach Bobby Knight in the parking lot!)

Bob Jones confers with Brutus Cheiftain of Poets In Distress.

The Olympic game between Brazil and Italy provided inspiration for the gig. During the game Brazil fans busted out with their chant, "Whoa-whoa- Brazil!" For the show, the band acquired a tape of the official Olympic theme music and entered Oscar's like it was the opening ceremony, high-fiving clubgoers as they filed in. Their first song was the Brazil chant, which led into the song "Mr. Fireworks", where Mr. P employed pyrotechnics for the first time, or at least tried to, as the sparkler he brought in took forever to light.

The show was recorded directly off the

Alan Waddington

Mr. P

Bob Jones plays "Desperation" guitar

mixing board and remains to this day an incredible document of the ragged, extraordinary sonic explosion that was the Squad at the time. For the Oscar's show the band had brought a keyboardist named Dave and brought back Ian Carlson to play trumpet. Jeff Hayes' guitar was buried in the mix as Bob Jones' erratic "Desperation" guitar was blasted. The combination of moody keyboard, Jones' guitar and occasional trumpet

Laura and Ian

Jeff Hayes

bursts on the one hand, and the solid rhythm provided by Hayes, Waddington and Laura Kovach as a counter balance, synthesized into territory later explored by groups like Sonic Youth. In 2012, the band made "Desperation Squad Live at Oscar's Cornhusker 1984" available online.

In the long run, Alan's involvement with The Unforgiven led to the band's first major personnel change. When The Unforgiven signed a contract with Elektra Records, Waddington left Desperation Squad and was replaced with 15-year old protégé, Ian Carlson.

Desperation Squad was only one of a number of bands emerging in the nascent mid-80s Pomona Valley music scene - a much more diverse polyglot than the underground punk scene that preceded it.

There were The Flamethrowers with Kurt Ross, Steve Alba, Jeff Moses, and Ed Neville; and Human Therapy with Mick Rhodes; and The Dull, who released a 45, "I Hate The Motorcyclist."

Alan was in a million bands. The Escorts had evolved into EMS with the addition of Hayes on bass (!) and vocals, along with Woodbury, Waddington and Hamm. EMS would go on to release an eponymous EP. Alan was also occasionally jamming with The Dull. Terry Churchman's band Silver Chalice featured guitarist and noted Dead Kennedys producer Geza X, Don Bolles on drums and the most flat out bat shit crazy singer on the circuit, the Wesson-oil swilling Kim Komet, who would use pliers to pull out pubic hairs on stage. Even Rod Curtis and Craig Herring had re-emerged with a new band, Suva.

There were three bands that would go on to play the biggest roles in the development of Desperation Squad.

One wasn't a band at all, rather the Poets in Distress, a renegade post-beat outfit formed after high school buddies Craig Rick and John Bender traveled to a poet retreat in Colorado and met Allen Ginsberg, who implored them to form their own group and to never approach or touch him ever again. Poets In Distress, which conducted bizarre ceremonies involving mead wine and sported aliases like Brutus Chieftain and

64

Kim Komet—Silver Chalice, 1985

Leader Sorcerer, seemed to exist only to vex D-Squad, disrupting their gigs, destroying equipment, and on occasion, attacking the band on stage.

Steve Jones, singer of the Stepmothers, was looking to form a new band with a more updated "Western" sound and contacted Alan to be his lieutenant, a stand-up drummer surrounded by the hunkiest players in the Inland Empire, playing songs seemingly all inspired by Clint Eastwood movies. Even the band name, The Unforgiven, was a movie title and would eventually become a Clint Eastwood movie as well. Featuring Just Jones on guitar, Mike Finn on bass, Johnny Hickman (who found success in Cracker with Camper Van Beethoven's David Lowery), and Kurt Ross' older brother Todd on lead guitars, and with catchy hook-filled songs like "Hang Em High" and "All Is Quiet On The Western Front", The Unforgiven's debut at the Music Machine in September 1984 was practically a coronation. This swaggering band from well east of L.A. came stomping into town and immediately became the subject of an intense major-label bidding war.

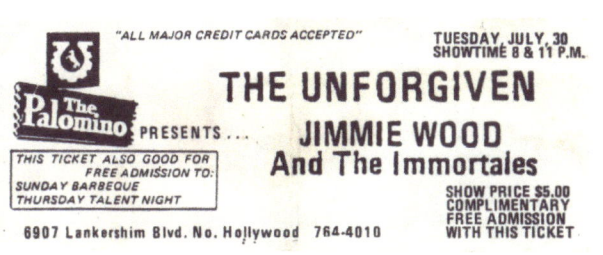

The Unforgiven didn't play gigs, they annihilated them, a brigade of screaming groupies at every show, many of them future Hollywood starlets. Guns N' Roses played one of their first shows opening for The Unforgiven. Shelly da Cunha, the gossip columnist for the L.A. Weekly, adored them and plugged them with regularity. The Unforgiven became the heart and soul of the new Pomona Valley rock scene, even if they rarely played in town. Still, the Unforgiven's power and animal magnetism created a scene practically by itself, giving Desperation Squad and all the other bands a platform they likely wouldn't have had otherwise, with kids going to shows in the hope of discovering the next Unforgiven.

Desperation Squad had much to prove.

In 1981, Dave Carpenter, Mark Givens and Joel Huschle formed Wckr Spgt. Carpenter left in 1982 to go to college, leaving the duo of Givens and Huschle to create a music world of their own. The two had been at it for a couple of years when Desperation Squad first encountered them at Madame Wong's West, on the same downstairs bill. This time it was Mr. P who stood and marveled at the lead singer, Huschle, more manic and ballsy than he.

November 1984

Watching Wckr Spgt play at Madame Wong's was a transformative experience — Givens' raunchy guitar, a drop dead gorgeous teen angel dressed in black on bass, and Huschle, bringing out a bowl of water, placing it on the stage, dripping to all fours and screaming "I drink water like a dog!"

It was band love at first sight. Squad and Spgt formed a creative alliance which saw much cross-band collaboration. Mr. P started spending a lot of time with Givens, listening to strange music by Autistic Mezas, The Crunch Sisters, and The Bloody Hawaiians, not realizing they were all essentially Givens and friends, and could all be traced back to the Love Bunnies.

Givens welcomed Mr. P to the greater Claremont community, tight-knit, like Diamond Bar, but with a vibrant downtown, the Village, where hip Claremont twenty-somethings congregated at various hang-outs: Rhino

Records, Some Crust Bakery, Rayne Beau Raggs, the Folk Music Center, Harvard Square or the tiny Bohemia of Nick's Caffé Trevi, where the Real Time Jazz Band held court, all this against the backdrop of the Claremont Colleges, which Desperation Squad would get to know intimately soon enough.

By entering Wckr Spgt's sphere, Desperation Squad automatically gained a robust following well beyond the Pomona borders, becoming as much of a Claremont band as any others of the time. Givens proved handy at graphic art as well, designing dozens of band gig fliers. To that point, Mr. P and Bob Jones handled most of the band flier work, Jones in his signature abstract style, Mr. P in his usual hit or miss style.

After attending "Spgtfest" in October of 1985 and becoming especially fond of the Wckr Spgt cassette "Drops of Love", Mr. P extended an invitation to Givens to join the band - playing a tiny Casio keyboard - just to add a bit of Spgt irreverence to the D-Squad mix. The move somewhat rankled the rest of the band, who didn't share Mr. P's appreciation of irreverence. Still, no could deny that the Wckr Spgt connection brought Desperation Squad many happy returns.

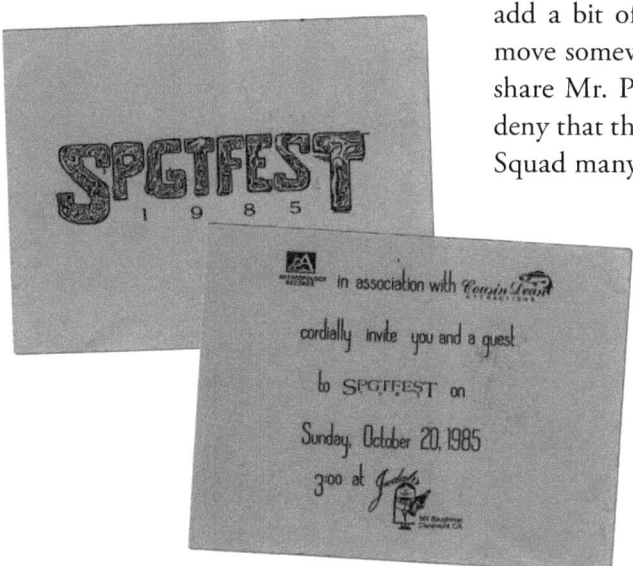

One lesson Mr. P learned from The Blortemus was that he should never pick up a musical instrument and play it - ever. He wanted the band to have an avant-garde edge and Bob more than filled that role, but there should be soft melodic elements as well. Elaine Donaldson was a family friend and former Music Plus employee who traveled from Kansas with bandmates, Dresden, to make it in L.A. She could also sing like an angel. She was D-Squad's first backup singer. Elaine proved a good fit for the band and lasted three or four gigs before bowing out.

Next into the mix came Caroline, Wckr Spgt's angel dressed in black, and Becky Hamm from EMS. At this time D-Squad was practicing at Arts Building, still hanging in there on the east end of 2nd Street. Becky and Caroline were both showing up to rehearse with the band, usually at different times, which seemed like a competition. Eventually they both joined the band and D-Squad had the biggest rarity on the club circuit - two female back-up singers. Caroline lasted a few months before she too stepped aside and Becky claimed the spot all for herself. During the Caroline-Becky era, a local photographer and friend named Donna Scriven came to numerous shows, as well as the band

rehearsal studio, Dragonville, to take some of the best shots of the emerging band, playful and unpretentious, a band that was having a lot of fun being a band.

As for Becky, she would eventually take the back-up position to great wailing, hand truck banging heights, becoming the band's most popular member and crowd draw.

By 1985 Art was looking to relocate the Building, leaving the downtown institution he had presided over for close to five years, the only venue both Nixon's Revenge and Desperation Squad appeared at. Desperation Squad had been rehearsing there but would have to find somewhere else to go.

In summer of 1985, the band practiced at Dragonville, located in an industrial park just south of Arrow Highway on White Avenue in Pomona. The women who ran Dragonville, Barb and Diane, were great early supporters of the band, but it too closed its doors towards the end of 1986.

An old friend from the Stratus days, Brett Solomon, alerted D-Squad of a loft he rented with a local sound engineer Tim Kirk (not the Tim Kirk from The Love Bunnies) that was located on the corner of 2nd Street and Garey Avenue in downtown Pomona above

the PIP Printing shop, whose owner knew Mr. P's dad when he had a print shop, Lawson Printing, just around the corner on 1st Street in the early 80s. One of Lawson Printing steady customers was Toxic Shock Records, itself two or three doors down on 1st Street.

Desperation Squad and Kirk took to each other so well that the band was soon laying down tracks in his studio. Eventually, Desperation Squad would inhabit this corner loft for the next seven years, until 1994. Additionally, Becky Hamm, who was also a prolific artist and art teacher, rented her own loft on near Main Street for roughly the same period.

Eventually Becky's place would become Space Gallery.

Desperation Squad's most enthusiastic fan base was by far the Claremont Colleges, where from 1985 to 1993 the band played countless shows across the 5-C "Ivy League of the West" campuses, with student support that sometimes bordered on mania, especially during Pomona College frat parties where they generally got paid based on how many beer kegs were consumed. It all started at a tiny coffee house at Scripps College, the Motley-to-the-View, in 1985, their reputation and stature growing to such mythical proportions that hardly a month went by without the Squad playing somewhere on campus, whether it be The Wash or Wed Nite (Pomona College), Appleby Beach (Claremont McKenna), senior art openings (Claremont Graduate School),

the Kohoutek Festival (Pitzer College), or a dorm party at Harvey Mudd. During this time, the band met Franklin Bruno, guitarist and songwriter from the band Nothing Painted Blue, then an undergraduate at Pomona, who on one occasion came up and sang along to a Pere Ubu cover with the Squad.

Forming Desperation Squad solved one of Mr. P's problems but didn't put any money in his pocket. In December of 1984 Mr. P walked into the Music Plus record store in Azusa and asked the manager if she was looking for Christmas help. The manager, Anna Bunch, just happened to a friend of Mr. P's and was in fact once hired by his brother John, who had been a Music Plus manager for years.

The symbiosis between Music Plus and the greater southern California music community was readily apparent well before Mr.P got a job there. All of the SoCal record stores - Licorice Pizza, Tower Records, even the much lamented Wherehouse - were staffed with dudes (and the occasional girl) in bands. Several Music Plus workmates would provide pivotal contributions to D-Squad.

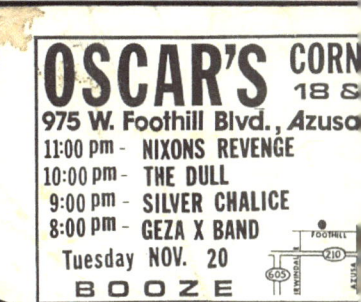

It was a lot of work but between work and band, Mr. P had in less than two years completely transformed himself from radio reject sad sack to coolest dude on the planet, making decent money at the Plus, gigging four or five times a month with the band, hanging out, doing blow, being "Mr. P" (most of the people he worked with at Music Plus had no idea his name was Kevin). It was the best of times.

Chuck Garcia was already employed at Azusa when Mr. P met him. Garcia, as it turns out, was an old high school buddy of Bob Jones, and a tremendous artist in his own right, doing cover art for the Silver Chalice LP. On his own

Garcia sketched out in pencil a band shot, which represented the band better than any photo had done up to that point.

Damon Shotwell was dubbed "The Alarm" because his hair greatly resembled the style worn by the band of the same name. Shotwell was a hotshot guitar player and played in a variety of bands. For a brief period in the early 90s "The Alarm" joined D-Squad as bass player.

But the most bizarre consequence of Mr. P working at Music Plus was his reuniting with old Stratus buddy and nemesis Bruce Watkins, who had been at the Plus for several years himself and replaced Anna Bunch as manager in Azusa in 1985.

It was a happy reunion. Though it had only been two or three years since the bust up of Stratus, it could have been 20 years.

Mr. P became an Assistant Manager and attended meetings at "#1", the Music Plus main office. Mr. P generally stayed quiet and just scribbled on his note pad. In case of musical inspiration, he had a column on one side of his note paper that simply said "Song Ideas". This day had yielded some songs with potential like "The Truck Is Coming", "Joe, The Brinks Man" and the presumably epic "Last Days of the Writedown Book".

Music Plus managers were the "hipsters" of their day, people just a little too full of themselves, and the meetings were like mini-coronations of their rarefied coolness, which is why everyone was caught off guard when up to the Music Plus podium came

MRP Halloween 1986
(Pants later stolen at Limbo Lounge)

Mr. P with "Grampa" Monster 1988

a diminutive older woman, rumored to the head of payroll, positively unhip and presumably harmless, a woman named Ethel.

Ethel proceeded to rip these stupid manager hipsters a new asshole so huge that some started cowering under their tables. Ethel screamed at the entire room about all the silly dumb mistakes "they" make every day that she had to fix. "You don't staple through the hard copy, do you hear me, you do not tape the change to the drop envelope! What about these microwave bills! The next person who tries to cash their check at a store by saying 'I'm from #1' I'll have you fired! I don't care who you are!"

It was so unnerving to those assembled that when Ethel finally left, Music Plus' resident hipster owner Dave Berkowitz had to come out and personally reassure his top brass that no one was going to fired, by Ethel or anyone else for that matter.

On his note pad under "Song Ideas" Mr. P wrote "My Name is Ethyl".

A day or two later Mr. P showed Watkins his notes. "My Name Is Ethyl" Bruce commanded. "That's the song you should write." It was by far the punkest number D-Squad had written ever. "There is one thing you gotta know - My Name Is Ethyl! My Name Is Ethyl! These are the rules and I run the show! My Name Is Ethyl! My Name Is Ethyl!" During the breakdown he detailed all of the unpleasantries that Ethyl had ranted about.

"My Name Is Ethyl" would go on to become one of the most popular Desperation Squad songs of all time, still in the starting lineup after 25 years. When the band needed to pick a new opener midway through the Warped Tour, "My Name Is Ethyl" filled the bill.

It became a big hit in Music Plus circles as well. The biggest fan? Ethel. Ethel thought the song was simply great.

Another person Mr. P met while working at Azusa was a young guy from Claremont who was the activities director just down the street at Citrus College named Kevin Lyman. Lyman would come in the store with fliers for upcoming shows and talk to Mr. P. One day Lyman asked his advice on whether to book an well-known but aging rock act or Howard Jones, who had just released his "Dream Into Action" LP. "Howard Jones is blowing out the door" replied Mr. P. Lyman booked Jones and the show was a huge success. As Mr. P would joke later, it was the last time Lyman ever took Mr. P's advice.

Mr. P worked at Music Plus four years, walking away in December 1988 to devote more time to Desperation Squad.

In early 1986, Pat Bacich was hunting all over the San Gabriel Valley for a new concert venue that could showcase local bands as well as bring in an occasional big-name headliner. The Fandango bar was a long-time C&W dive that was headed towards oblivion, sharing a valuable piece of real estate across from the Montclair Plaza with a rundown and mostly vacant motel and a roller rink. A match was made.

Though Desperation Squad had played a gig there with The Flamethrowers and Rik L Rik in February, the "Grand Opening" of the Fandango in March featured L.A. glam band extraordinaire Poison and The Unforgiven who were at that moment recording their first LP for Elecktra Records, **In October, the Fandango changed its name to the Green Door,** evoking visions of cheesy 70s porno, and for the next five years the Green Door in Montclair was ground zero for the Pomona Valley/Inland Empire music scene. It was an incredibly eclectic

place where rock legends (Bo Diddley, Blue Cheer), indie stalwarts (Camper Van Beethoven, They Might Be Giants) and regional up-and-comers (The Honky Tonk Angels, Rozzi Lane, Psych 201, Rude Boy) all mingled together in a wildly popular milieu that was vibrant, vital and enduring. Bacich had a knack for attracting viable headliners and a soft spot for breaking new bands.

Quite often a Green Door bill would feature four seemingly mismatched local acts that somehow fit. Before pay-to-play decimated the L.A. rock scene, Green Door was notable for loyal, entertainment-starved kids who would arrive early, leave late, and consume lots of alcohol. Desperation Squad was remarkable in that their sound was almost completely impervious to stereotyping - they weren't a roots band, a punk band or a metal band, yet their good-natured wackiness allowed them to get placed on any bill and fit in. They were equally at ease with Poets in Distress as

they were with The Flys, or The Minutemen, or Bad Religion. Very quickly, Desperation Squad became the Green Door's "fun" band, dazzling the crowds with dopey/intense songs like "I Died In An Auto Accident", "Breaking Nobody's Heart" and "Great Big Boogers Of Love". Of all the band members, it was singer Becky Hamm, whose strong pipes and virtuoso hand-truck banging commanded the most attention, and allowed D-Squad to transition from club favorites to the next Big Thing, a band who could get away with playing weird music for normal people.

One night in late fall 1986, Mark Givens took Mr. P over to his parent's house in Claremont and, as they stood in the garage, gave him a present, something given to him by Bob Fritz, something Mr. P could use on stage: **a handcrafted Panda mask**. Mr. P thanked Mark for the wonderful gift and tried it on. It was an odd fit. It was made of heavy fabric, with no air holes for the nose, just a large opening at the mouth. Wearing it for more than five minutes would be next to impossible because of the discomfort. Yet, the mask was adorable. It could and would be incorporated into the act in some fashion.

Panda Man was born.

If there is one universal image of Desperation Squad, it is Panda Man. Panda Man at the Limbo Lounge. Panda Man at the Green Door. Panda Man at the Wash. Panda Man on the steps of City Hall on Election Night. Panda Man on the Warped Tour. Panda Man at the Fillmore. Panda Man cavorting with Regis Philbin. Panda Man shaking his butt at Comic-Con. Naked Panda Man on the pages of the Los Angeles Weekly.

Panda Man was not around during the Arts Building days, true. And the idea of an iconic Panda Man took a while to develop. But the moment Mr. P put the mask on, he was no longer Mr. P, he was Panda Man, and Desperation Squad fans loved Panda Man.

The Panda "head" became the band's logo, also created by Givens, and among the rare collectibles in the D-Squad universe are the Panda t-shirts made for the "Hot Diggitty Dogs" roll out.

There are two Panda masks. The original was used until 2001, when a newer, sturdier mask was taken on the Warped Tour (the original was in fragile shape and Mr. P was convinced that it would get lost forever on the road). The Warped Tour also saw a "junior" Panda mask for the crotch.

For 30 years Panda Man has been Desperation Squad's mascot and best known figure. Long live Panda Man!

For a short period the Limbo Lounge was the hippest place in Los Angeles to play. Emanating from the Four Star Saloon, an old-school, battered drag bar wedged between a new generation of brightly-lit, techno-filled gay bars cropping up on Santa Monica Blvd., the Limbo Lounge played host to bizarro performance artists including Glen Meadmore, Nova China and the Goddess Bunny. Prominent among the wacky characters was Danny Hernandez, another of Darlene Waddington's buddies from Mt. Sac, now known professionally as Danielle, an emerging underground figure in L.A. and old friend of Desperation Squad. Danny happily arranged a booking for the band there, where for the first time, they encountered cultural shock. (Indeed, the

first person they saw as they entered the Four Star was Goddess Bunny, being pawed over by a drunk patron.)

1987 was a year of change for the band. To this point, they had been genial amusing hipsters, with goofy and popular songs like "Great Big Boogers (Of Love)". Despite this, Mr. P noticed that crowds were starting to tune out, that the D-Squad live show was possibly too quirky and avant-garde. A more streamlined energetic set was required.

Mr. P had already written a powerful new rocker, "I Need A Girl (With A Car)" and wanted to augment it with like-minded material. In a burst of creative energy, he wrote four new songs and the band debuted them all at a special show at the Limbo Lounge.

"Serious Love" was possibly the best-arranged and tightest song Desperation Squad ever conceived. The lyrics centered on a lovestruck man who would endure any manner of pain - getting beaten up by cops, smashing his hand in a mirror, even dancing "like a spaz" and hitting his head with a lunch box. Why? Because it was serious. Serious Love. The dual guitar riff by Hayes and Jones, along with the propulsive rhythm by Carlson and Kovach made "Serious Love" as catchy as "Puppet Man" but way more rocking.

Danny Hernandez and Patricia Morice at the Limbo Lounge

DESPERATION SQUAD

at the LIMBO LOUNGE
MAY 21, 1987
9:00

"Me and My Drug Problem" chided not only those who tried to pass off their habits as merely casual aberrations but also the Nancy Reagan inspired "Just Say No" campaign, blending the two with humor and power.

"Cindy", the band's first true ballad, hooked crowds immediately with its dangling "Cindy I want your hole - some love" lyric. The frat-rocker "Skull" pondered the despair of arriving at a party with "1600 scammasters" and only one girl.

These four songs, along with the fast-food fantasy "The Woman Who Sleeps with Jack" and two cover songs, were unveiled at a much-hyped gig at the Limbo Lounge. The new material propelled the band to greater heights. The same could not be said for the flowery new thrift store pants Mr. P wore that night, stolen from his prop trash can after the show. Dismayed, D-Squad never played the Limbo Lounge again. The new songs, however, propelled the band to newer and greater heights.

> **Cindy**
> Cindy, you are my soul
> Cindy, my rock and roll
> Cindy, I want your whole—
> some love
> Please, teller please teller
>
> Cindy, I'm not afraid
> Cindy, don't go away
> Cindy, I want to lay—
> down the rules
> Please, teller please teller
>
> This is not a calcium deposit
> Though I want it white
> I don't have cholrine in my eyes
> But that's what it smells like
> Doesn't it
>
> Cindy, a piece of cake
> Cindy, a dream to make
> Cindy, I want to break
> up your marriage

SEVEN

As Squad worked its way through the various stages of band existence they began to consider whether they would produce their own LP or, as was becoming increasingly popular among bands at that time, a demo cassette to sell at gigs.

Tim Kirk, the sound engineer, worked with the band to hone their sound. D-Squad had at this point done a handful of demo sessions, but in 1987 they had a solid three years of material to choose from. Kirk and the band started with 8-track recordings of "Puppet Man" the Tom Jones cover that was a huge crowd favorite, and Mr. P's surprise hit "Girls Piss Me Off",

which real live girls found to be cute and hilarious, demonstrating how far Mr. P had come in his songwriting development, now that bitter and angry could be repurposed as smart and funny.

Both songs came off well. The group continued to fine tune their new songs and one night during a rehearsal Tim Kirk flicked a switch and recorded the band live on 4-track, just to get an idea what to do during a later session. Becky was not present this night, just Mr. P, Jeff, Bob, Laura, Ian and Mark.

It was a good session, inspired playing and witty banter from Mr. P and Jeff between songs. When listening to the tracks a few days later, Mr. P and Kirk came to the same conclusion - the tracks were dynamite, recording the band live captured their spirit better than standard tracking and what they recorded sounded like a whole Side One of a record just as it was. If they could record a Side Two even half as good as the first they'd have enough to sell at gigs.

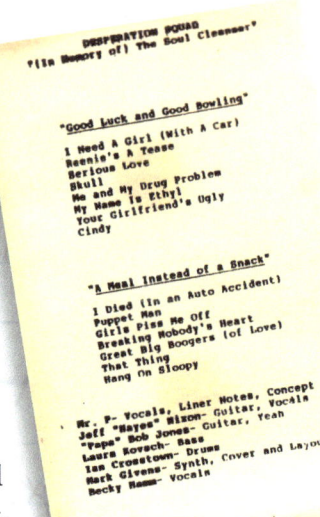

There was one glaring omission - Becky missing from the entire Side One. But if there was a lesson to be learned from the Nixon's Revenge days, it was to go with what you had. The short-handed tracks remained.

"The 'Go with what you have' strategy would prove useful for Desperation Squad. The very day of the Side Two recording, the band was invited to make a music video at a mobile video recording studio located somewhere in Pomona. The invitation was so last minute that only a few band members could be rounded up to appear at the shoot - Mr. P, Ian, Becky and Mark. No Hayes or Laura or Bob Jones. How would they pull this off?

Since the band was only lip-synching along to the tracks ("Girls Piss Me Off" and "Puppet Man"), they put Mark on bass, recruited Henry Barnes of Amps For Christ (with the Panda mask on) for one guitar, and good friend Howard Drucker who stood in for Bob Jones and who, with a hat, shades and goatee, looked so similar to Bob that only D-Squad aficionados could tell the difference.

Later that night, the audio recording session went as well as it needed to, a hodgepodge of older tracks with one or two surprising omissions – "Looking Good" which they were no longer playing, and the devastating fashion rant "You Look Stupid."

"(In Memory Of) The Soul Cleanser" consisted of 15 songs, 60 minutes of unadulterated Desperation Squad. It was released in February 1988.

IN MEMORY OF
THE SOUL CLEANSER

D-Squad was gigging everywhere at the time, including at the Green Door with the one indie band they matched up well with — fIREHOSE. The two bands ended up doing four shows together at the Green Door. With the fIREHOSE gigs and the release of "Soul Cleanser", the band was experiencing their highest level of popularity. Yet the band was about to go through one of its most jarring changes and really, no one saw it coming.

Tension had been mounting and arguments were on the rise within the band. Somehow, peace would need to be restored for the band to continue their ascent. Clearly, a change had to be made.

Dave Carpenter had graduated from Yale and was back in Claremont. The Squad could use Carpenter in the band, if only to bring harmony back to practices and gigs.

Carpenter came into the group as advertised, a solid bass player willing to put in extra work to learn all of the D-Squad set list. His first gig was a rare two-fer, a gig at Rhino Records in the afternoon and a Claremont Colleges toga party that night. Carpenter pulled it off. D-Squad fans missed Laura and were confused but they were also supportive. Carpenter was in and the band was ready to take things to the next level.

1989 was a watershed year for Desperation Squad. With "Soul Cleanser" providing momentum, the band began playing with more frequency in Hollywood at such hot spots as the Coconut Teaszer, the Central, and especially the Whisky-A-Go-Go, where they became regulars on the No-Bozo Jam Night, a multi-band showcase where acts would play 15 minute sets on a shared backline. This somewhat dubious premise proved for D-Squad a revelation, as their hyper-kinetic energy and extraordinary presence blew away both crowds and bands alike.

Desperation Squad was also receiving a great deal of press, popping up in a variety of places - college newspapers, local fashion mags, and Hollywood rock zines. Where most Pomona Valley/Inland Empire bands were seeking to identify with particular trends - hair band, cowboy band, post-punk band - Desperation Squad's unique act made them a textbook paradox: fresh enough to be unable to pigeonhole, but too different to take a chance on.

November 22, 1989

Trying to acquire record company interest was frustrating and ineffective, especially for a band living on the outskirts of L.A.

Into this void came their old friends, Kevin Lyman, now a stage manager for the SoCal-based promoter Goldenvoice; and Ray Woodbury, now guitarist and road manager for the David Lindley band. Lyman and Woodbury approached Desperation Squad with a proposition: would they want to join their fledgling record company and record their very first CD?

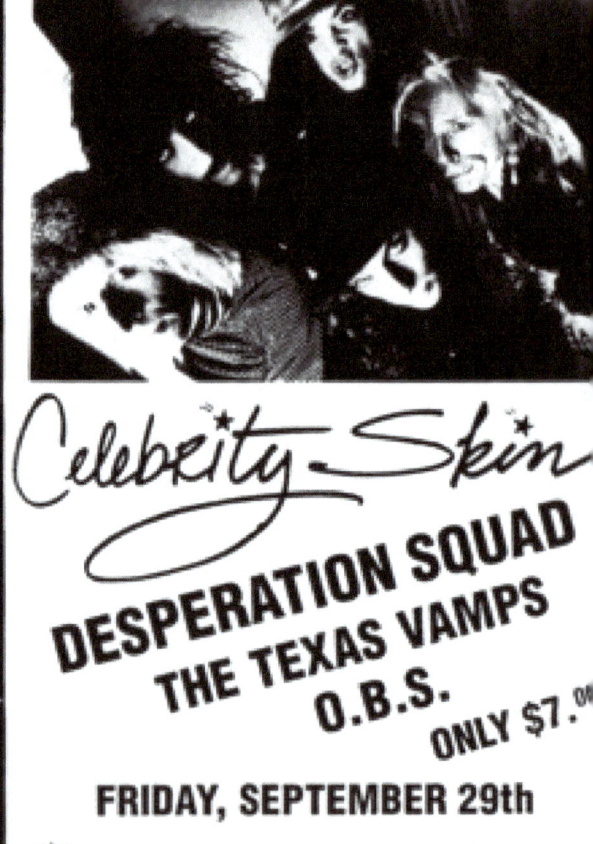

Outer Space Records was the brainchild of Ray Woodbury and Kevin Lyman who, like Desperation Squad, were looking to take things to the next level. Their proposal to the band was simple: find investors to finance a CD, then use their connections and savvy to market the band and, best case scenario, sign them to a major label deal. An investors prospectus was drafted, identifying the principals and finance structure, and also hyping the band's potential - "a popular and busy band on the college and club circuit in Southern California". This was certainly true as 1989 was proving to be D-Squad's highest profile year to date, their show ascension never yet hitting a speedbump. Desperation Squad was on the way up and industry backing was just the thing to push it all over the top.

What transpired, however, was much different. Confusion, delays, miscommunication and questionable strategies doomed the project almost from the start.

Channeling the energy from "Soul Cleanser", the CD was also recorded "live" in one session at Indian Hill Recording in Claremont, direct to digital with no extra tracking or overdubs. The resulting 17-hour marathon pushed the band to the breaking point, blowing Mr. P's voice out and putting a severe strain on the entire band.

D-Squad virtually disappeared from live performance, one exception being a Nick's Caffé Trevi show attended by local Claremont musician Ben Harper, who heard the band perform the hard-charging rocker "Lonesome Train". And there were delays with the release of the CD, pushing the date into the summer, well after the Claremont Colleges graduation. In 1990, the year *Hot Diggitty Dogs* was released, Desperation Squad had hung out with the graduating class their entire time at the colleges. The Class of 1990 were easily the most devoted Squad fans of all-time and they missed the release of the CD by two weeks.

"99% of bands that got signed in the 80s could tell basically the same story of record company meddling and incompetence. The difference for Desperation Squad was that we weren't dealing with coked-

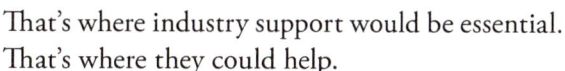

up number-crunching suits, we were dealing with longtime friends who we trusted with our future. They were our common sense saviors that were going to solve all of our problems. And our problem wasn't whether we could play or not, it was whether we could ever find our audience, national or otherwise.

That's where industry support would be essential. That's where they could help.

"They put together this northern California tour that started with a roadtrip to Santa Cruz to play the Catalyst, and some girl leads us to the dressing room and there's a cooler of beers and we're new, we don't want to make waves, we ask her politely, "who are the beers for?" And she's getting ready to walk out the door, stops and turns around and says very logically, "the beers are for the main band" and we're like COOL! And that's the story behind the song "Band!",

93

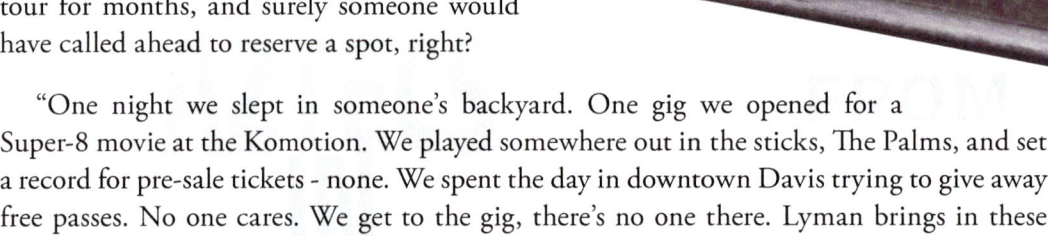

that's where that came from, "Beers for the main band!" So there we are, D-Squad, drinking all the beers, play two sets with Dread Zeppelin, fucking rock, rock hard, a long day. A long long day. By the time we get to our campground, – not motel, campground – and we pull into the campground well after midnight and it's, like, sold out! The campground is sold out. But that can't be, because we've been planning this tour for months, and surely someone would have called ahead to reserve a spot, right?

"One night we slept in someone's backyard. One gig we opened for a Super-8 movie at the Komotion. We played somewhere out in the sticks, The Palms, and set a record for pre-sale tickets - none. We spent the day in downtown Davis trying to give away free passes. No one cares. We get to the gig, there's no one there. Lyman brings in these two kids who were just passing through town and volunteered to open for us, the gig with no people, and they turn out to be Mecca Normal, then a half dozen Pomona College students wander in, and that's the gig.

"The tour was a disaster.

"Here's the problem: We trusted these people. I personally trusted them. They had extraordinary

vision. I believed them. I believed they could do it. Our job was to rock. That's what we did. Their job was to roll out the CD, find our audience, and make the goddamn campground reservation!

"The tour ended with a truly bizarre show, again at the Catalyst, where we drove 10 hours to open for Social Distortion, got flipped off by our audience - two mohawk sporting punk kids - drove 10 hours back home, and that was it for the summer.

"Then in September we played a show in front of 2,000 people and blew out Social Distortion at Cal Poly Pomona. It was a fluke but we did it. I still get people coming up to me to this day, telling me that was the greatest gig they had ever seen in their life. The next day we went to the Foundations Forum Heavy Metal Convention in LA and raised hell there and did a killer showcase. That weekend we could

POP MUSIC REVIEW
Squad Cranks With Delightful, Wild Abandon

By JIM WASHBURN

WESTMINSTER—Perhaps all of us are haunted by those shows that got away, legendary one-time events that occurred while we were somewhere else. While others worry about missing Springsteen in a biker bar or Peter Gabriel at the Bear, for well over a decade this writer has been irked about missing an Orange County group called Gumby at Costa Mesa's killed-in-action Cuckoo's Nest.

According to those who were there, Gumby's performance was a fearless merger of art and utter ineptitude. Over the sort of pure dissonance that only the unschooled can create, the group's singer reportedly spent one song flailing about, clutching his forehead and pathetically repeating, "Mom, I hurt my head!" as catsup oozed from his hair. For a finale, the band hurled partially eaten sandwiches into the audience.

have easily been the hottest band on the planet.

"A mere three months later, we played our 7th annual Christmas show at Munchies, a sandwich place in the Pomona Mall. How nice it was for us to come back and play a hometown show! But it wasn't a visit. We were home - for good. Outer Space Records was over. In three short months we had gone from world-beaters to washed-up.

"But Desperation Squad was different and that was obvious from the beginning. And everything we did after that — that should have merited some attention but was passed over — everything we did after that, *that's* what makes Desperation Squad the greatest band of all time."

UNSIGNED BANDS SHOWCASING

DESPERATION SQUAD
What Is This?
A singer wears a panda head, dances in a spastic motion and sings about problems, drug problems and evil people named Ethyl. A girl, in lieu of standard percussion, beats on hand trucks and hubcaps. Bright colors attack from all sides. You're rocking hard but something's different. You're laughing hard. You've never seen anything like this before. One question remains
Who Are These Guys?
These guys are Desperation Squad, scourge of the Pomona Valley, champions of the ludicrous, purveyors of all things fun. They are something special. And Mr. P, lead singer of the band, sounds this sobering note:
"We're easily the funniest band around", he boasts, then warns, "now it's time to take us seriously."

Munchies was a sandwich bar by day, and new music hangout at night, drawing a surprising number of up and coming indie bands in their earliest stages like Weezer, the Mountain Goats and Ethel Meatplow, among many others.

For the most part, Munchies booked local bands. Ian Carlson and Jerry O'Sullivan formed The Streetcleaners in 1989 as a Diamond Bar party band, but quickly established themselves as the house band at Munchies, which happened to be down the street from the rehearsal place on 2nd in Pomona. The Streetcleaners even shared the rehearsal loft with Desperation Squad and the two bands enjoyed many successful shows at Munchies.

After the release of "Hot Diggitty Dogs" and the Outer Space Records tour, Desperation Squad returned home and got back to work, with an eye on a new record deal. D-Squad had relied for years on songs that were basically live performance pieces first,

album tracks second. Funny songs that caught people's attention but didn't necessarily translate well in the recording process. The new focus would be on songs that had more commercial potential and would work well in the studio.

It was one of the best periods of new music ever in Desperation Squad. "Common Law Woman", "Bomb Factory Baby", "The Girl Was Tall", "Now That I'm A Fox", "Cute Little College Girl", and especially "Now I Want to Have Sex With You" were part of a complete overhaul of D-Squad's set that worried less about stage antics than foreseeing a future where people would come to the show wanting to hear the cool songs they dug from the CD. It was a noble effort. In practice though it didn't work out so well.

In the effort to reinvent itself, Desperation Squad's cachet as a monster live band took a hit. Crowds weren't as keen on the band if they weren't going to play "Girl With A Car" anymore.

Dave Carpenter left the band to pursue a writing partnership with former bandmate Tim Kirk. This left a void in the bass player position that the

ROCK AND ROLL WILL NEVER SMELL THE SAME

saturday, november 23rd

band found itself continually trying to fill. Damon "The Alarm" Shotwell gave it a shot, but this arrangement didn't work so well.

Dave got a gig freelancing for the Los Angeles Weekly and pitched them a piece about the Inland Empire music scene, where he would talk up numerous local bands, his former bandmates included. In October of 1991 L.A.-based photographer Fredrik Nilsen traveled to Pomona to shoot D-Squad for the article.

Another odd development was the formation of a new band with Just Jones and Mike Finn, who asked Mr. P if he wanted to sing. The resulting group, named Bung Boy, was primarily a vehicle for Jones' songs. When they played their first gig at Munchies in September of 1991, Ian was the drummer. Bung Boy recorded a fairly decent six-song demo and would somehow inexplicably wind up with their picture on the front page of BAM magazine.

The final show at the Green Door showed just how much Desperation Squad had slipped locally. Pat Bacich wanted to book as many bands in one night as he possibly could, so every band save for headliners The Honky Tonk Angels, another Kurt Ross-fronted band, played disappointingly short sets.

With new bass player Dan Scratch, Desperation Squad tried valiantly to postpone

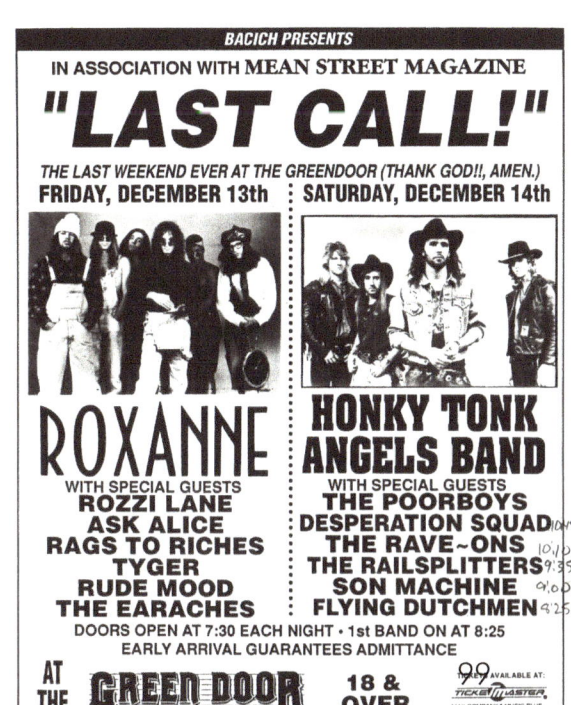

the inevitable but gig opportunities were drying up. Goldenvoice wouldn't book them for any LA shows, so it really was just Munchies and an occasional show at the Ice Thai out in Hollywood, where they were booked to play a big show with the Mentors. In the end, the show was a disaster. The Mentors didn't bother to show up.

There was one person who still believed in the band, journalist Melinda Lewis, who wrote two articles on the band in 1992, one for Factor X magazine and the other for Mean Street. That March 1992 piece finally showed the cracks in the band coming to the surface. It was revealed the band was trying to make it's own movie titled "Not The Doors" but nothing came of this.

Try as they might Desperation Squad just couldn't get their groove back. They had been together now for over eight years, an eternity in band years. Stratus was around barely four years. Same with The Unforgiven. Now they were getting shoved aside by local promoters and local bands, and even their own rehearsal studio mates.

If Desperation Squad had quit here, no one could have blamed them and they would have acquitted themselves well and had nothing to be ashamed about. Theirs was the typical band story. They weren't the typical band in the typical story, yet they were going to end their

careers the same way every other band did, with barely a whimper, let alone a bang.

But Desperation Squad didn't go out with a whimper, and the implications of their last act would be felt for decades to come. In a way, it's where the whole idea of "Desperation Squad as Art Collective" coalesced and it started when Mr. P filed papers in the City of Pomona mayoral primary, scheduled for March 1993.

The Rock and Roll Mayor Campaign was born.

Ballot with a Beat

Guess where they're really rocking the vote? Would you believe Pomona? The mayoral race for the city, located about 30 miles east of Los Angeles, could give new meaning to that cheesy Starship song, "We Built This City on Rock 'n' Roll." It's all riding on the candidacy of Mr. P, lead singer of Desperation Squad.

You won't hear Mr. P mouthing trite slogans like, "P for Pomona, P for Prosperity." There are seven other candidates eager to plow that tired old turf. Instead, Mr. P exhorts his fellow citizens to "get some rock 'n' roll into this town, ya know?"

"When I am elected Mayor of Pomona," he adds, "we'll put a state-of-the-art sound system in the mayor's office and just crank tunes all day." P promises that any band, from anywhere in the country, can come to the mayor's office and drop off a tape. What about spoken word and mutant industrial stick-breaking (not to mention grungecore and Wilson Phillips)? "Well, I use the term 'bands' loosely; you can interpret it any way you want. I want people all over the country to know they can drop off a tape in Pomona.

"Seems to me it's the least I can do for the city."

If you're not eligible to vote in Pomona, you can still show your support by purchasing Desperation Squad's new cassette single, "I Am the Mayor (The Rock & Roll Mayor)/Soy El Alcalde (El Alcalde de Rock & Roll)."

— Gary Holt

A sound initiative: If Mr. P is elected mayor of Pomona, he promises to install a mega stereo in City Hall and "crank tunes all day."

the Noise / March 1993   9

ON THE RECORD

"I want the kids to vote for the rock and roll mayor. I want their parents to vote against me."

—Rock musician **Kevin C. Ausmus**, who, billing himself professionally as Mr. P, is one of eight candidates for Pomona mayor. **J1**

Mr. P had been living with his mom and brother in a rented house in north Pomona and, as always, looking for a way to jump start the band. He found it one day in late 1992, in a Daily Bulletin piece on the upcoming Pomona mayoral election. Mr. P wondered how difficult it would be to get on the ballot. As it turned out, no application fee and a petition signed by twenty registered city voters made you a candidate.

Thus started the Rock and Roll Mayor Campaign,
a publicity lark by a fringe candidate that would change the political and civic landscape of the city and pave the way for thousands of bands to be welcomed to the city's neglected downtown.

From Arts Building to the P.V.A. to "Soul Cleanser" to Becky's loft to the dA Gallery to Munchies, D-Squad's history had been played out on or around the vicinity of 2nd Street in downtown for close to 13 years. If anyone could speak for the underground musicians and artists, certainly it was Mr. P.

Downtown had been a ghost town for as long as anyone could remember. Once one of the country's first open air malls, with department stores and restaurants, by 1992 it was mostly low-end antique shops and band rehearsal spaces with a few code-violating artist lofts thrown in.

City politics and civic morale were at an all-time low, the city council mired in increasingly polarizing and personal disputes, with combative players like three-time incumbent mayor Donna Smith, recently recalled Clay Bryant and bickering council members Nell Soto and Tomas Ursua presiding over a city with a record number of homicides and an embarrassing, failed multi-million dollar world trade center - nothing more than a weed-strewn vacant lot at the corner of Mission and Garey, just two blocks from the D-Squad rehearsal studio.

After filing papers, Mr. P prepared a press release which he hand delivered to the two newspaper beat writers covering the election - David Fondler of the Daily Bulletin and Mike Ward of the L.A. Times. Fondler had profiled the state of Pomona's downtown arts scene the previous summer - Becky Hamm was one of its subjects, as was Chris Toovey of the dA Gallery - and described the city's interest in it as little more than ambivalent. Both responded by profiling the rock singer prominently, the Times going as far as breaking out his "I want the kids to vote for the rock and roll mayor, I want their parents to vote against me." quote in its On The Record feature.

Election results
All 26 precincts reporting
Results are unofficial

Pomona - Mayor	Votes	%
Kevin "Mr. P" Ausmus	96	1.4
*Eddie Cortez	1,690	25.0
Paul Geiger	1,599	23.7
James Reynolds	41	0.06
Ramon Romero	203	3.0
David Smith	253	3.7
*Tomas Ursua	2,600	38.5
James Wilkins	263	3.8

Pomona - City Council		
District 2		
Marco Robles	621	100.0
District 3		
Boyd Bredenkamp	319	42.7
Cristina Carrizosa	428	57.3
Albert Midgette	12	0.0
District 5		
Donald Andrews	0	0.0
Elliott Rothman	395	34.8
Ken West	739	65.2

* Run off election between these two candidates will be held April 20, 1993

Kent Salas/Daily Bulletin

Candidates for mayor
Kevin Ausmus

Born: Oct. 14, 1959
Residence: off and on for 15 years
Occupation: rock 'n' roll singer
Company/employer: The Desperation Squad band
Background: active in the local music and arts community for years; attended school in Pomona; involved in radio station and drama at Mt. SAC and community theater; founding member of the band Nixon's Revenge; was singing with the band Bad Attitude on stage when punks trashed the former Pomona skateland, "a legendary gig," in 1980.

	Business retention and development	Graffiti, gangs and youth
Kevin Ausmus	Favors building up the downtown artist and entertainment community with clubs and shops. "It seems every city around here has got something. La Verne has that big movie theater, Rancho is getting a baseball team."	Favors a community effort to encourage people to volunteer to clean up their own neighborhood. "The first step is not to make the mistake that every kid that's got a Kings hat on is a gang member."

D-Squad quickly assembled at Steve Santamaria's, guitarist for The Streetcleaners, studio to record "I Am The Mayor (The Rock and Roll Mayor)" for release in time for the February Candidate's Forum. Channeling the city's demographics, the cassette's flip side contained a poorly enunciated Spanish language version "Soy Es Alcalde (Alcalde De Rock and Roll)".

The Pomona Central Business District, comprised mostly of curmudgeonly antique store owners, held an informal get together for the candidates. Mr. P started his speech by reminding them his father Gene was once one of them, a downtown business owner. From there, Mr. P launched into a frenzied appeal to downtown artists and bands, which was summed up by the District this way:

"Mr. Ausmus feels that there is nothing to draw people to the city, that there needs to be more emphasis on entertainment establishments."

This was a sentiment likely posited by many others would-be entrepreneurs over the last dozen or so years. The difference was that Mr. P was a candidate for public office and was thereby presenting this fairly obvious need as a political issue. Mr. P was picking the locks that had barred any sort of comprehensive downtown arts and music plan for years.

It was the Candidates Forum where Mr. P, in the words of David Fondler of the Daily Bulletin, stole the show. The mayoral primary brought forth a host of first-time candidates, most of whom were political novices. A palpable air of tension braced the auditorium.

Pomona politics had been so acrimonious for the last several years, no one could remember when there had been a light moment, let alone huge belly laughs. Mr. P provided these and more, conducting a forum that was part stand-up, part improv, part

DO NOT VOTE IN PAMPHLET. USE BALLOT CARD ONLY.

1-M OFFICIAL BALLOT - CITY OF POMONA PRIMARY NOMINATING ELECTION - MARCH 2, 1993	
For MAYOR	Vote for ONE
DAVID W. SMITH Engineering Administrator/Designer	2 → ○
RAMON P. ROMERO Deputy Sheriff Supervisor	3 → ○
JAMES ROBERT REYNOLDS Horseman/Instructor	4 → ○
TOMAS URSUA Vice-Mayor	5 → ○
EDDIE CORTEZ Business Owner	6 → ○
KEVIN "MR. P" AUSMUS Writer/Performer/Musician	7 → ○
PAUL D. GEIGER Aerospace Engineering Manager	8 → ○
JAMES WILKINS Planning Commissioner	9 → ○

Aquí vemos a Cortez discutiendo algunas estrategias con Romero

civics lesson that the rest of the nervous candidates were grateful to hear - it made them feel much more at ease.

Mr. P's opening statement was the "Mad as Hell" monologue from the movie "Network". His campaign promise was to "bring a boom box to the mayor's office and crank tunes all day". He chided city officials for ignoring the downtown underground arts and music community, stating that if Pomona youth were encouraged to pursue the arts they might stay off the streets. Mr. P cracked jokes, invited bands from all over the country to come drop off a demo at City Hall, plugged the band cassette and showed no interest at all in any issue that couldn't rock out. "Issues! You gotta love em but they just get in my way".

Mr. P wasn't finished. He and Martin Kauper got together and filmed a number of 30-second ads that ran incessantly on local cable. Campaign signs were made. A Daily Bulletin candidates Q&A featured a wild-eyed long-haired photo of Mr. P (taken by Walt Weis), and his views of "Business Retention and Development" - "Favors building up the downtown artist and entertainment community with clubs and shops."

Again, these weren't necessarily original thoughts, but placed in the context of a city election, they were practically revolutionary. No one else who favored these developments had gone this route before, and this included several very interested Pomona downtown property owners and outside business interests.

When Election Day finally rolled around, a couple dozen supporters gathered at the D-Squad rehearsal loft and prepared to march on City Hall, parading down 2nd Street, making a few stops along the way to muster up more support. Inside city chambers Mr. P got some startling news - despite tons of publicity his vote total was less than a hundred. Fringe candidates that had nothing to offer the city were trouncing him. As he joked later, at least he beat the homeless guy. He garnered 1.4 percent of the vote. Good guy gas station owner Eddie Cortez would eventually be elected in a runoff with runner-up Tomas Ursua.

Outside, D-Squad geared up to play "I Am The Mayor" on the steps of City Hall. With the crowd chanting, the Panda mask came out and all at once, it was over.

Later that night, back at the studio, Dan Scratch told Mr. P he was quitting the band, once again leaving D-Squad without a bass player.

What started in May 1984 on a pick-up truck was seemingly running aground close to nine years later. D-Squad played one more gig - without a bass player - at the Motley at Scripps College and slowly, almost imperceptibly, faded away. It had been a long haul with a lot of good times and a few bitter disappointments. It was, in the end, the typical band story.

Within a year, a sign was erected on 2nd Street in Pomona. It said "Arts Colony". Art galleries and lofts began to sprout up all over the place. The downtown area began to show signs of life. In 1996, the Glass House opened and thousands of bands would be welcomed to the city's revitalized downtown.

> The remaining votes were divided among the rest of the pack, including James Wilkins, David Smith, Ramon Romero, Kevin "Mr. P" Ausmus and James Reynolds.
> As officials with the city clerk's office posted the totals through the night, a pattern quickly became apparent, with Ursua leading throughout and Cortez and Geiger in a neck-and-neck race for second.
> While the votes were being counted, Ausmus' rock band Desperation Squad began loudly playing "The Rock and Roll Mayor" on the steps of the council chambers where the votes were being counted.
> Ursua contacted at a nearby restau-

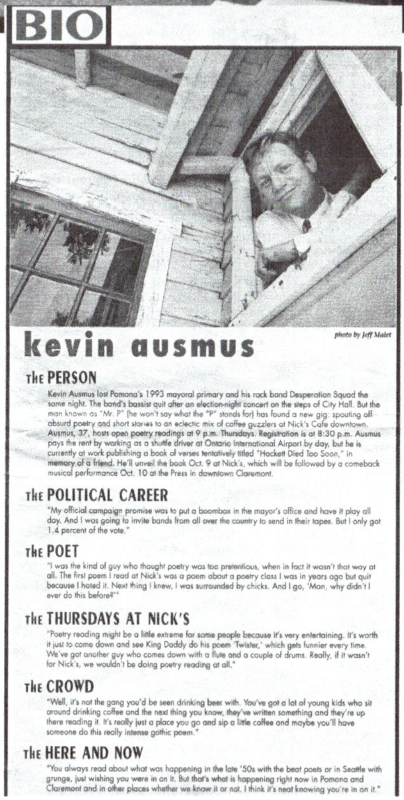

kevin ausmus
photo by Jeff Malet

The PERSON
Kevin Ausmus lost Pomona's 1993 mayoral primary and his rock band Desperation Squad the same night. The band's bassist quit after an election-night concert on the steps of City Hall. But the man known as "Mr. P" (he won't say what the "P" stands for) has found a new gig: spouting all absurd poetry and short stories to an eclectic mix of coffee guzzlers at Nick's Cafe downtown. Ausmus, 37, hosts open poetry readings at 9 p.m. Thursdays. Registration is at 8:30 p.m. Ausmus pays the rent by working as a shuttle driver at Ontario International Airport by day, but he is currently at work publishing a book of verses tentatively titled "Hackett Died Too Soon," in memory of a friend. He'll unveil the book Oct. 9 at Nick's, which will be followed by a comeback musical performance Oct. 10 at the Press in downtown Claremont.

The POLITICAL CAREER
"My official campaign promise was to put a boombox in the mayor's office and have it play all day. And I was going to invite bands from all over the country to send in their tapes. But I only got 1.4 percent of the vote."

The POET
"I was the kind of guy who thought poetry was too pretentious, when in fact it wasn't that way at all. The first poem I read at Nick's was a poem about a poetry class I was in years ago but quit because I hated it. Next thing I knew, I was surrounded by chicks. And I go, 'Man, why didn't I ever do this before?'"

The THURSDAYS AT NICK'S
"Poetry reading might be a little extreme for some people because it's very entertaining. It's worth it just to come down and see King Daddy do his poem 'Twister,' which gets funnier every time. We've got another guy who comes down with a flute and a couple of drums. Really, if it wasn't for Nick's, we wouldn't be doing poetry reading at all."

The CROWD
"Well, it's not the gang you'd be seen drinking beer with. You've got a lot of young kids who sit around drinking coffee and the next thing you know, they've written something and they're up there reading it. It's really just a place you go and sip a little coffee and maybe you'll have someone do this really intense gothic poem."

The HERE AND NOW
"You always read about what was happening in the late '50s with the beat poets or in Seattle with grunge, just wishing you were in on it. But that's what is happening right now in Pomona and Claremont and in other places whether we know it or not. I think it's neat knowing you're in on it."

Desperation Squad had been inactive for over four years when Mr. P became the regular host of an open mike poetry night at Nick's Caffé Trevi in Claremont. Poetry Night directly spearheaded a Poet's In Distress revival, with new member that included King Daddy, his wife Betty Nude and Mr. P himself.

During this time Mr. P wrote a poem called "Taco Truck" based on a real-life experience in Pasadena with Bob Jones and Charles Garcia. "Taco Truck" became emblematic of the new creative direction engendered by the Poetry Night, which evolved into a standing room only success. At it's peak, Poetry Night was

profiled by the Inland Vally Daily Bulletin and also the poetry circuit zine "Next...". The newly revived PID made numerous appearances, including the 1998 Doo Dah parade, the same year Mr. P issued his chapbook "Hackett Died Too Soon."

In Oct. 1997, Mr. P staged a show at The Press restaurant in Claremont. Bung Boy opened the show followed by the "Mr. P Band", who played the first music version of "Taco Truck". The end of the show found the classic Desperation Squad lineup - Mr. P, Hayes, Bob, Laura, Ian, and Becky - together on stage for the first time in over four years.

Slowly over the course of 1998, a resurgent Desperation Squad took hold, playing their first formal show since 1993 at The Old Towne Pub in Pasadena. The Pub would act as a home base for the next two years.

MR. P & FRIENDS
a live music performance
IDAY, OCT. 10 - 9:30 p.

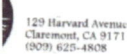

In 1999 Alan Waddington and Jeff Hayes found themselves on the Warped Tour as part of the Inland Empire Orchestra, a band comprised mainly of Citrus College jazz musicians. Hayes was the lead singer. Upon their return Hayes told the band about Warped acts like Eminem, Lit and Blink 182, which sounded a lot like the early moronic songs of early Desperation Squad.

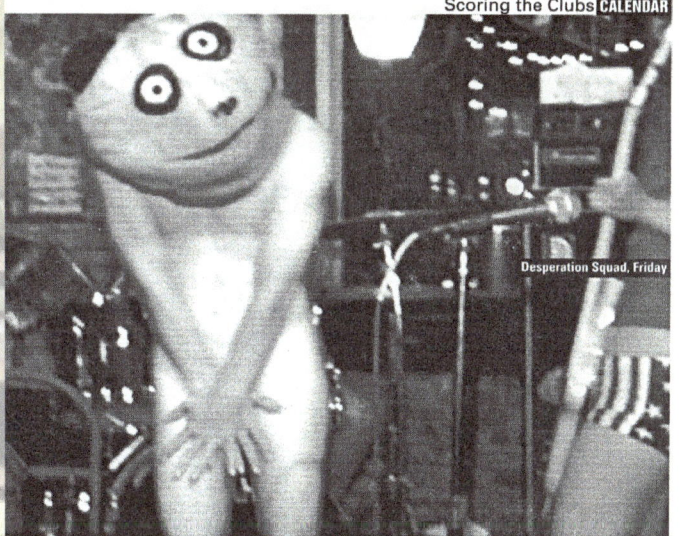

If they were to compete with bands half their age, they had to be twice as outrageous. Mr. P came up with the song idea that would shape and define the band's sound in the new millennium, "The Best Ass In Rock And Roll."

At the end of a rather lackluster show at The Old Towne Pub in Sept. 1999, Mr. P donned the Panda mask and tore off the rest of his clothes, dancing naked for several minutes. A picture of "Naked Panda Man" would eventually make its way to the LA Weekly, promoting their first show at Mr. T's Bowl in Feb. 2000.

Desperation Squad's "new" sound could be traced directly to its Nixon's Revenge roots. The long-awaited "I'm An Asshole (For Rock And Roll)" was finally developed. A song Mr. P wrote when he

was 10 years old, "Get It On", retitled "Jello Ball" was added. After some experimentation, "Me And My Drug Problem" acquired messy food props. Mr. P started sporting a leopard spotted thong. And Desperation Squad dug all the way back to the Nixon's Revenge San Dimas backyard party gig to revive Brian Waddington's "We Ain't Getting No Pussy Tonight."

There was one disappointment, the departure of Becky, who stepped aside just as this new entirely brazen and altogether shocking new act began to hit its stride. Led by a by a string-bikini clad Laura Kovach and Mr. P who began using his physique shamelessly as a performance tool. It was time for Desperation Squad to go on the road.

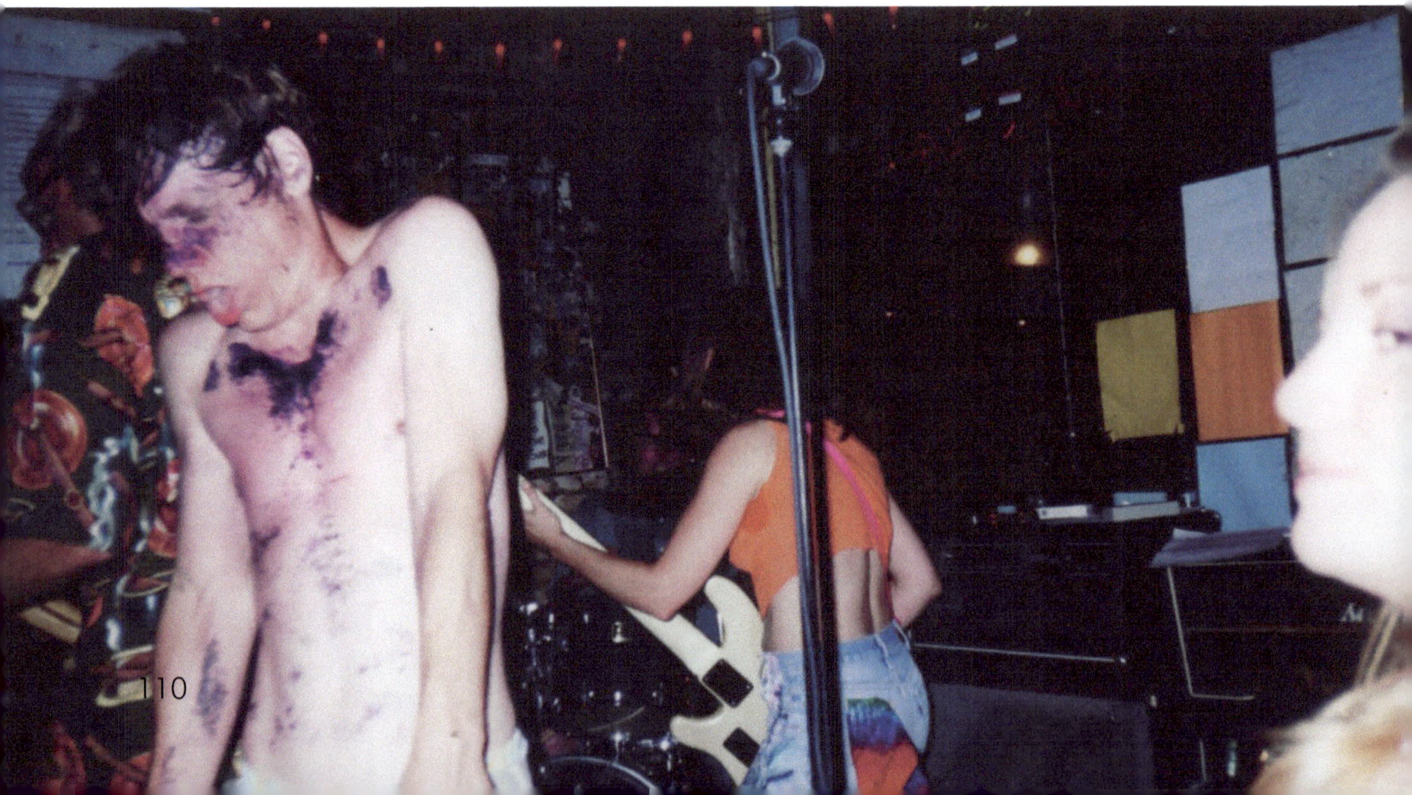

Desperation Squad performs at Irvine Meadows Amphitheater, at a show that featured the B-52s and The Pretenders.

In February 2001, Mr. P received an email from Kevin Lyman, who in the years since Outer Space Records, had founded the Warped Tour. "Is the band busy this summer?" Lyman asked. Out of nowhere, Desperation Squad was preparing for their first national tour, with a once-in-a-lifetime deal - all-access passes, meal passes, per diem for the whole band and free passage on a tour bus. (It was the same deal the Inland Empire Orchestra received.)

Lyman's grand plan for the band was to pair them with the '01 Warped Tour's signature act, The Incredibly Strange Wrestlers from San Francisco, whose Lucha Libre on acid punk rock blowouts at the Fillmore had made them Bay Area legends. Lyman's idea was for Desperation Squad to perform music during the wrestling matches. One problem: Lyman had not consulted the wrestlers or their hard-nosed manager Audra

111

Morse. Morse refused to go along with the plan. Suddenly, the band's invitation was in danger of being revoked. Desperation Squad quickly pledged to Lyman their support one way or the other. Mr. P also reached out to The Incredibly Strange Wrestlers and Morse and managed to clear the air, even traveling up to San Francisco with Alan Waddington to catch an Incredibly Strange Wrestlers show at the Fillmore. It was there Mr. P first saw the spectacle of hundreds of crazed fans hurling tortillas at a wrestling ring, a tactic Desperation Squad would later co-opt for their own stage show, with oftentimes contentious results.

Desperation Squad quickly assembled in the studio of Mike Gonzales, who had gotten his start running sound with The Unforgiven and since had become a prominent sound engineer. The result was "This Is Our Demo" or simply "The Warped Tour CD", which included "Band", "Jello Ball", "I'm An Asshole For Rock And Roll", "Taco Truck", "No Pussy Tonight" and "The Best Ass In Rock And Roll".

Unbeknownst to the band, Kevin Lyman was having problems finding a tour bus to place them, again putting the tour in jeopardy. At the last minute Lyman placed them aboard Bus #6, the "Set-Up" or "Merch" bus. This placement would have dire implications for the band.

Desperation Squad had a short and controversial stay on Warped Tour bus #6. The band's busmates were mostly corporate reps for sponsors like Ernie Ball or Alternative Press or members of the set-up crew, many of whom thought the band were thieves and lowlifes. D-Squad tried hard to make friends and fit in as best they could.

The Warped Tour program listed D-Squad as passengers on Bus 8, the "Motox" bus that carried the daredevil "Balls of Steel" kids, who defied gravity and common sense by cycling at high speeds inside a steel cage. This arrangement was quickly scuttled by the kid's parents and another bus had to be found to carry the band. Two days before the tour began in Phoenix, Bus 6 was chosen for the band, a modus vivendi that did not work out.

THE WARPED TOUR

Another obstacle for Desperation Squad was finding a stage for them to play on. In 2001 there were four "main" stages that were more or less taken over by the headline acts. The guitar string manufacturer Ernie Ball sponsored a booth and a regional battle of the bands contest. The winning bands got to play on the Ernie Ball stage at their local Warped Tour. This is the stage that D-Squad called home for the duration of the tour, playing in an out of the way area of the tour grounds, on what Cleveland Scene newspaper would later describe as "the equivalent of the back of a pick-up truck." None of this mattered to the band, as they quickly adapted and made fast friends with Mike the sound man and his assistant.

> **ON THE ROAD WITH THE SQUAD** - June 26, 2001
>
> *"What is rock and roll? Rock and roll is playing in the 115 degree heat in Las Vegas while Rancid is playing in the air-conditioned Thomas & Mack Center and still having someone say you are the greatest band of all time. Rock and Roll is having kids who win free passes to Warped back stage wanting autographs even when you tell them you are the the least known band on the tour. Rock and Roll is Jimmy the bus driver. Rock and Roll is having people hoot at you and screaming 'you rock!' while you are walking back to the venue with a 30-pack of Keystone. Rock and Roll is not having time to tell you about rock and roll because you are too busy doing it!"*

After a whirlwind first day on tour, the band retired to Bus 6 for the overnight trip from Phoenix to Las Vegas. Before they alighted in Vegas D-Squad had managed to cause enough of a drunken ruckus that the band was threatened with dismissal. A heated bus meeting was held

The last thing Desperation Squad expected to find at their bus in Fresno was a booze and gambling party

to clear the air and it seemed as if the worst of it had blown over.

The next stop was Fresno, where the band first met Shonali Bhowmik of the Atlanta band Ultra Baby Fat, who played on the Ladies Lounge stage located next to the Ernie Ball stage. The Ladies Lounge hosted a rotating schedule of female-fronted bands like Bottom, Lo-Ball, the Halo Friendlies and, oddly, the all-male Sugarcult. The set-up crew was in the midst of a booze and gambling party, shotgunning beer bongs and playing dice games. In fact, the tour had hit a rare

115

two day off period, which the merch crew was taking advantage of. It seemed as if an olive branch had been offered, as the band was invited to join up in the revelry. With two days off in San Diego and the hometown Los Angeles gig awaiting, it appeared that all ill will had been dissolved.

Los Angeles marked the end of the first week of Warped Tour, the hometown show. Dozens of drunken D-Squad supporters showed up for a Bus 6 back stage party. It was a festive day.

Mr. P ventured out to watch indie bands they had become pals with like User Friendly from San Diego, and The Benjamins from Milwaukee. Along the way one of the wrestlers stopped to inform him that D-Squad was

Desperation Squad shares a light moment, shortly after being dismissed from their tour bus and driven home in a stretch limousine.

now "The Official Band of the Incredibly Strange Wrestlers". The timing could not have been more ironic. Midway through the party, Kevin Lyman arrived to inform the band they were being dismissed from the bus and would be driven home in a stretch limousine.

Desperation Squad's time on the Warped Tour was over, their first national tour getting them no further east from Phoenix. The gloom that descended gave rise briefly to a twisted sense of accomplishment - that of being "Invited To Leave", a lyric from "Asshole For Rock And Roll" - and then to sheer numbness. As a salve, Lyman paid the band the entire summer's per diem.

Thinking quickly, Mr. P asked Lyman, "We're only kicked off the bus, right? We're not kicked off the tour." Lyman expressed tremendous support for their return to the tour if they could provide their own transportation. Desperation Squad said goodbye to as many people as they could, got in the limo and went home.

ON THE ROAD WITH THE SQUAD II - June 27, 2001

"It has been determined by bands as diverse as Jones, Ultra Baby Fat and the Incredibly Strange Wrestlers that we are the best band on the Warped Tour. This is in only four days. ...but like the Power Aid guy said, 'Drink it or throw it out!'"

After their untimely dismissal from the tour, Desperation Squad hunkered down and retooled, determined to find a way to get back on the road. The solution was to rent a Ford Expedition with a luggage rack, then attempt the almost 700 mile journey to Salt Lake City. The trip began ominously as several bags flew off the top of the Expedition on the I-10 freeway in Ontario. Then the band had to endure three separate flash floods as they drove north straight into the teeth of a Rocky Mountain summer storm. They finally stopped for the night in Fillmore, Utah.

Now off the bus and on the road, Desperation Squad had to find nightly accommodations. The close quarters - long drives after the show and a tiny motel room to fit all five of them - chipped away at band morale and kept everyone in a constant state of agitation.

D-Squad with their friend from Claremont, rapper Woes Hinzo, who worked catering.

Fortunately, all this tension had no effect on stage, where the band's outrageous antics and solid musicianship combined to reward those adventurous enough to seek out the Ernie Ball stage with the spectacle of a flesh-baring, mask-wearing, thong-sporting, age-challenged act, where virtually every song centered on some part of the human anatomy, all leading to the thrilling finale of the Panda Man/

Ultra Baby Fat, from Atlanta, with singers Michelle Williams and Shonali Bhowmik, were among the first fervent D-Squad supoorters

119

Bikini Girl wrestling match. In the days before social media, the band's triumphs were limited to only the time and place where they happened, so instead of crowds coming to the tour anticipating a new and crazy act, every tour stop required a new hustling up of a crowd.

Through trial and error, Desperation Squad adapted and revised their set list to maximize its impact and minimize "walk-aways", concert-goers who would stop and watch the band for a minute and then leave. The first casualty was "Girl With A Car", a longtime fan favorite that proved too long and unwieldy

---

SQUAD TRIUMPH ON THE WARPED TOUR - June 30, 2001

ON THE ROAD WITH THE SQUAD

"...In a whirlwind week, with as many twists and turns as a Golden Oldies dance party, The Desperation Squad achieved its ultimate triumph barely days into the 2001 Warped Tour - being proclaimed "official" band of the Incredibly Strange Wrestlers of San Francisco. Ladies and gentlemen, this was no easy victory and shows what the power of live performance can do for you..."

---

for punk rockers. "Feel Like Makin' Love", used as a bridge to "Your Girlfriend's Ugly", suffered the same fate. Oddly, even "Taco Truck" had to be scuttled because, in the pre-tortilla tossing days, it wasn't a compelling enough song to hold the crowd. This left the band in a bit of a bind. They had seven solid songs. Also, if Mr. P donned the Panda mask before the show and walked among the crowd yelling "come see the weird band!",

> **SQUAD TRIUMPH ON THE WARPED TOUR**   -   *June 30, 2001*
>
> *"...Oh, and you may have heard about something else in Los Angeles and I will clear this up for you so rumors don't run out of control. It seems we are having an unscheduled interruption in our touring. Due to "Acts Committed While Being A Band" we have been invited to leave our tour bus, effective immediately after the Los Angeles show. But we went with class and dignity, being driven home (with all our gear) elegantly in a stretch limo. In any case, this is only a minor glitch, just a temporary fly in the ointment, as we plan to resume the tour in Salt Lake City, pulling up in our own custom Winnebago, where we will return as conquering heroes I'm sure. We know the wrestlers will be glad to see us! And all the hard-working people in Bus 6 will be able to get all the sleep they deserve. Believe me, it's better this way...."*

they could draw enough interest from bored bystanders. They needed a short opening song that could utilize the Panda mask without suffocating Mr. P in the intense midday heat and humidity. It was decided to bring back "My Name Is Ethyl" to open the show, giving D-Squad a solid 27 minutes of punk rock that would eventually draw and hold huge crowds.

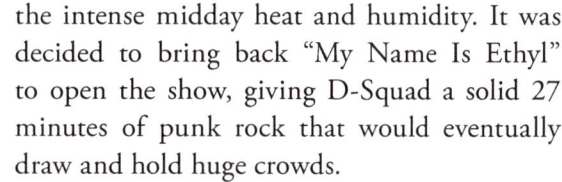

At the show in Somerset, Wisconsin right outside of Minneapolis, where they built a special stage to accommodate Blink 182's only 2001 appearance on the tour, Mr. P met Scott Olson, a photographer free-lancing for Rolling Stone. Olsen took two amazing photos for Rolling Stone's online "Say Cheese" photo essay, which included 311, The Vandals, The Ataris and many of the other big name acts on tour that year. The "Say Cheese" subtitle: "Blink 182, Fenix TX, Desperation Squad and New Found Glory bring the Warped Tour to Wisconsin", appeared above every band picture, giving the impression that D-Squad was itself one of those headline acts.

The Randall Island show in New York was a huge dust bowl that found Desperation Squad at the peak of their performance powers. Once again, the visually compelling D-Squad dominated the online photo album of the magazine NYRock with two pictures of a bikini-clad Laura and a series of pictures of Mr. P in various states of outrageousness.

After the Chicago show, Kevin Lyman told the band they had been seen by two high powered music industry movers and shakers, Gary Gersh and John Silva - managers of the Beastie Boys, Foo Fighters and Tenacious D - whose reaction to their performance was "Who the hell is that crazy Panda mask?" Lyman gave a copy of their CD to Gersh. The next year, Jack Black introduced a new Tenacious D song with the oddly-familiar title, "Taco Truck From Hell".

Desperation Squad received no heroes welcome when they returned home from the Warped Tour in early August 2001. Their first show back wound up being a completely pointless show at the Universal Bar and Grill in L.A. on August 23, where the band arrived to find no P.A. and no D-Squad fans.

Leave it to their new friends, the Incredibly Strange Wrestlers, to save the day by inviting D-Squad to the Incredibly Strange Wrestlers' own homecoming show at the Fillmore, gleefully titled "Homomania" on Oct. 11, where they found themselves on a bill with The Queers and the Fabulous Disasters. Desperation Squad also booked a show on Oct. 10 at the Pitzer College Gold Student Center with F-Word and the Lipstick Pickups.

Having been to an Incredibly Strange Wrestlers show prior to the summer, Mr. P knew the band would be pelted with tortillas at the Fillmore show and decided it would be a great idea to "gear up" for that show by introducing tortillas at the Gold Center show, naturally during "Taco Truck". It proved to be a huge, if messy, crowd pleaser. From that moment tortillas became a permanent part of the live act, which would prove to have polarizing and dire effects for the band in the future.

The Fillmore show was nothing short of spectacular. Arriving at the venue and embracing its great history - seeing the iconic posters adorning the walls - the band realized that this was a moment to be cherished. The band swaggered on stage to ringmaster

Count Dante's exuberant introduction and played mostly the Warped Tour set, the highlights being a ridiculously funny version of "No Pussy Tonight" and the hectic finale "Your Girlfriend's Ugly" with a Panda Man/Bikini Girl wrestling match for the ages. Rog Franklin, the Incredibly Strange Wrestlers' official photographer, documented the night for posterity.

DougMiller managed to reunite D-Squad with their Warped Tour buddies, the Angry Amputees, at a New Years 2002 show in Santa Barbara. In truth, the Amputees (whose bass player Dalty, was an amputee) and the Squad never met during the Warped Tour, but became fast friends at the New Years gig, which would lead to a hilarious adventure a few months later when D-Squad was invited back to S.F. to play Stinky's Peep Show on a bill with Youth Brigade on March 21.

It was Spring Break for Mr. P, who stuck around the Bay Area for a few days and spent one

crazy night with Joann and Dalty from the Angry Amputees, hopscotching from S.F. to Oakland, watching bands, getting hammered, and hoping to hook up with Sugarcult, who were playing at Slim's (where D-Squad had played back in 1990). Earlier in the evening, while waiting for the two in front of Slim's, Mr. P had a bizarre confrontation with an unknown member of a tour bus parked on the street, who struck Mr. P in the head with a megaphone. A security guard who witnessed the attack gave Mr. P the opportunity to press charges, which he laughed off, saying, "it's just a band thing".

Much later in the night, Mr. P, Joann, Dalty, and Dalty's girlfriend returned to the scene of the crime, and wound up on the same bus where the confrontation occurred. Mr. P begged to be dropped off before the return visit - The Angry Amputees had thought he was joking about the incident - but there he was, back on the bus and grilling a member of Sugarcult (who was visiting the bus as well) when Joann emerged from the back of the bus saying only, "we have to leave now." Mr. P's presence had been found out, prompting a hasty exodus, made laughingly absurd considering Dalty was confined to a wheelchair, which had to folded up and taken off the bus, then Dalty carried down the steps and placed back in the wheelchair. Outside, the drunken and

rowdy Dalty flashed his penis at the bus, causing the band to rush out with intent to harm. Mr. P and the others scampered to their truck, again having to gently lift Dalty out of his wheelchair and inside the vehicle, as the band and others chased after them with bottles.

All in all, Mr. P had managed to get kicked off a second tour bus in less than a year. Back at home a few nights later, while watching an episode of the Late Late Show with Craig Kilborn, Mr. P could have sworn he recognized the special musical guests from somewhere but couldn't be sure. They didn't have bottles in their hands, after all.

In 2002, Desperation Squad was editor's pick "Best Band of the Year" for Pasadena Weekly's year-end "Best Of…" issue, which netted them, among other things, free food and booze at the PW year-end party, and a slick banner they displayed at the Doo Dah Parade later that year.

editor's pick

BEST BAND
Desperation Squad

It's about the music, man — not the filthy Panda head and matching thong underwear singer Kevin P wears onstage during a show, or the brightly colored bikinis worn by bassist Laura Kovach or the animal-like thrashings of guitarists Bob Jones, Jeff Hayes and drummer Ian Carlson when the band performs on any given night. Desperation Squad's sound is as hard-hitting as their stage presence, and just plain good ol' sweaty rock 'n roll.

In March 2003, **Desperation Squad was contacted by Mike Odd, singer for the shock-prop band Rosemary's Billygoat,** who the band had gigged with at Mr. T's Bowl back in 2000. Odd asked the band to open his "Odd Art Show" at an industrial warehouse in Los Angeles called Qtopia's. Also on the bill were several other costume prop bands like Joe and the Chickenheads (later renamed The Radioactive Chickenheads) and the legendary Green Jello.

It was an odd fit for D-Squad since, aside from the appearance of Panda Man at the end of the show, their performance was not augmented by huge larger than life props and costumes.

The show was one of D-Squad's best ever, helped along by a huge crowd waiting for the doors to open. The sheer absurdity of a Desperation Squad - including the crazy Panda Man/Bikini

Girl wrestling match, which had evolved into a jaw-dropping spectacle of a finale - was photographed expertly by Sue Lawler, the designer of the 2000 Panda mask.

The Chickenheads had to follow D-Squad that night and vowed to never play after the D-Squad again. The Chickenheads and Desperation Squad would gig together several times over the years, and The Chickenheads always opened. This was a common refrain in the 2000s - Third Grade Teacher insisted on it, too. But for D-Squad, though this was the biggest compliment you could pay a band, it was a strategy that worked against the band, especially at L.A. shows, where club-goers unfamiliar with the band generally left in droves instead of sticking around to see the craziness.

Desperation Squad made one new fan at the Qtopia's show. Joe Black was a Pomona concert promoter who had just partnered with L.A. based graphic artist Rolo Castillo to open a new concert venue/art gallery.

Black and Castillo asked D-Squad to play a monthly residency at their new venue on

2nd Street in Pomona they were calling "51 Buckingham". The band hadn't played a downtown Pomona show since the Munchies days.

The first show was a grand affair, another show with Rosemary's Billygoat. After that, the shows were so poorly attended that they acquired a dubious nickname, "Tank Gig Saturdays". Poor luck plagued the shows. The Oct. 25, 2003 show occurred the same day as the outbreak of the notorious "Old Fire", one of the most devastating wildfires in California history. Smoke and ashes enveloped Pomona downtown. The usually bustling weekend art scene was completely deserted. The band played but there was no one there to watch it.

One noteworthy show came after 51 Buckingham had relocated across the street. Desperation Squad appeared with Shiragirl, a female punk duo from New Jersey who arrived in Pomona in a shocking pink RV emblazoned with the band logo on both sides. The bassist was a hired hand from Pomona, Vidal Lepe, who Mr. P had met a couple of years earlier when he played guitar for the Mega Muscle Pussys, a band fronted by Nupur Pandey, a regular from the Open Mike Poetry Nights at Nick's Caffé Trevi.

Mr. P spent the night hanging out with Shiragirl and wound up accompanying them as they crashed the 2004 Warped Tour in Fullerton, writing about it for Digress Magazine. The publisher of Digress Magazine was Annie Knight, a.k.a. "Mabel", one of several Riverside college kids introduced to D-Squad by yet *another* Poetry Night alumna, Alaska Quilici, who booked the band for the inaugural Gyroscope Collective Art Fair back in February 2002.

Knight was a burlesque aficionado and occasional performer. She invited Mr. P to attend the Super Bowl of burlesque, the 2003 "Tease-O-Rama" in Los Angeles. Acquiring a press packet, Mr. P was stunned to find a publicity photo for Charlotte La Bella Araigne'e, who was in fact Mr. P's longtime friend and upstairs neighbor, Tonia Bodley.

A month later, Mr. P formally introduced Annie to Tonia and practically on the spot the two quickly hatched the idea to stage their own burlesque show and form their own troupe, The Rambling Roses, with local performer Pepper La Rue and fashion designer Alison Sumner (who also fronted the shock band Whorrified).

"Burlesque Bash 2004" opened January 25 at 51 Buckingham, one night after a particularly dismal "Tank Gig Saturday". Annie brought Panda Man into her act and

he got the thrill of performing burlesque (although he had been for years in the D-Squad) and getting tied up on stage by the fetching Mabel.

Jeff Hayes suddenly quit Desperation Squad in February 2004, at the end of a band practice. This wasn't entirely unexpected. There had been tension in the band since even before the Warped Tour.

In 2000, after his first trip to the Warped Tour with the Inland Empire Orchestra, Hayes joined forces with Jerry O'Sullivan to form the band Rex Holmes, with Laura on bass, Tracy Robar (from the 80s band Psych 201 and guitarist in Bung Boy) on guitar and Brian Wells on drums. Hayes was spending more time with Rex Holmes and less time with D-Squad, promoting the new band and becoming local Claremont favorites.

Though D-Squad continued to play and develop new material, the band tea leaves seemed to indicate another long hiatus or even a break-up.

COME AND WITNESS THE MOST UNFORESEEN
BURLESQUE BASH OF 2004
AS ANNIE KNIGHT OF DIGRESS MAGAZINE PRESENTS TO YOU
THE RAMBLING ROSES AND GUESTS!

Featuring The Rambling Roses: Charlotte LaBelle, Pepper LaRue, and Mable
Plus the rock 'n roll of Leland's Cactus Ranch
And Alison Sumner's fashion show "Cold-Cocked!"

SUNDAY, JANUARY 25TH 8-10pm

@ 51 Buckingham
301 W. 2nd Street
in the Pomona Arts Colony
$5 cover
Sorry kids, 18 and over only!
For more info, email Mable at digress@9250x.com

Laura hung with the band for another year, wearing string bikinis and wrestling on stage with Mr. P, before she too left. In one year's time, two original members had left Desperation Squad, leaving them a trio - Mr. P, Ian and Bob. Had they decided to pack it in at this time - and many thought they would - they could still look back proudly at 20 years of being a kick-ass band with plenty of accomplishments.

But no one wanted to quit. Mr. P knew of a bass player, another in the long Citrus College pipeline, the easy-going J.P. Maramba, who joined the band in the summer of 2005, just in time, it turned out, for yet another abrupt zag in the band's fortunes.

Desperation Squad's resurrection in 1998 brought with it a new band element - the message t-shirt. The first such shirt was a plain white tee that Mr. P had crudely written "Fun Is Back" on the front. This was the new band motto - a new era, an old friend trusted with bringing back the good times - or put more succinctly in the next shirt, "Everybody Gets Laid" which was soon followed by "We Sell Beer."

In the summer of 2000 a new, shockingly direct message emerged: "Eat My Fuck", a historic meme that came to Desperation Squad's attention through "The Decline of Western Civilization."

The "Eat My Fuck" shirts were a huge hit from the start and one afternoon, a month or two before the Warped Tour, Bob and Laura and Sue Lawler gathered at Laura's pad in Temple City, made a stencil of the phrase in huge block letters, and spray painted it on the front of an undershirt. On a summer tour where even the most esteemed punk personalities bowed in puzzled reverence to this truly enigmatic band, it was the "EMF" shirt that was the most respected part of their absurd aura.

This reverence overlapped into the real world in February 2002 when, after a show at Zen Sushi in Los Angeles, Mr. P was approached by the proprietor of a trendy Hollywood clothes shop, Blest Boutique, who wanted

Mar 19 2004 4:59 PM EST

Courtney Love At NY Show: 'I'm Not Having A Nervous Breakdown'

Singer rants about legal problems, strips, rasps through set.

By Jennifer Vineyard

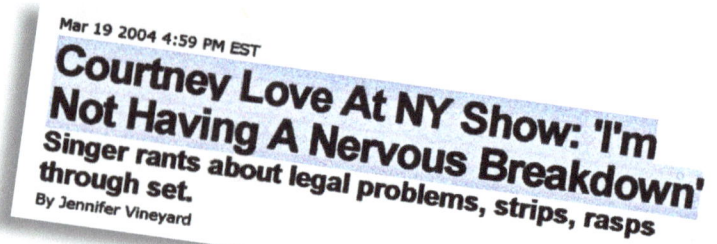

to buy a couple of shirts. Located just south of Hollywood Blvd. on Cahuenga, Blest was rumored to be patronized by the likes of Courtney Love.

It was a truly surprising moment a full two years later when Love herself walked out on the Bowery Stage in New York with one of those "Eat My Fuck" bad boys beaming defiantly to all who showed up to watch her latest meltdown. Approximately half those in attendance had cameras, and within days of the event Love's picture was everywhere on the internet, certainly the 2004 version of viral. The print media picked up on it as well, with Rolling Stone, Zink, Q (Britain), and Public (France), tossing it in the center of their snarky Love write-ups, with the pièce de résistance snark in some way channeling Love's foul-messaged shirt.

And it was a Desperation Squad shirt. They still had the stencil.

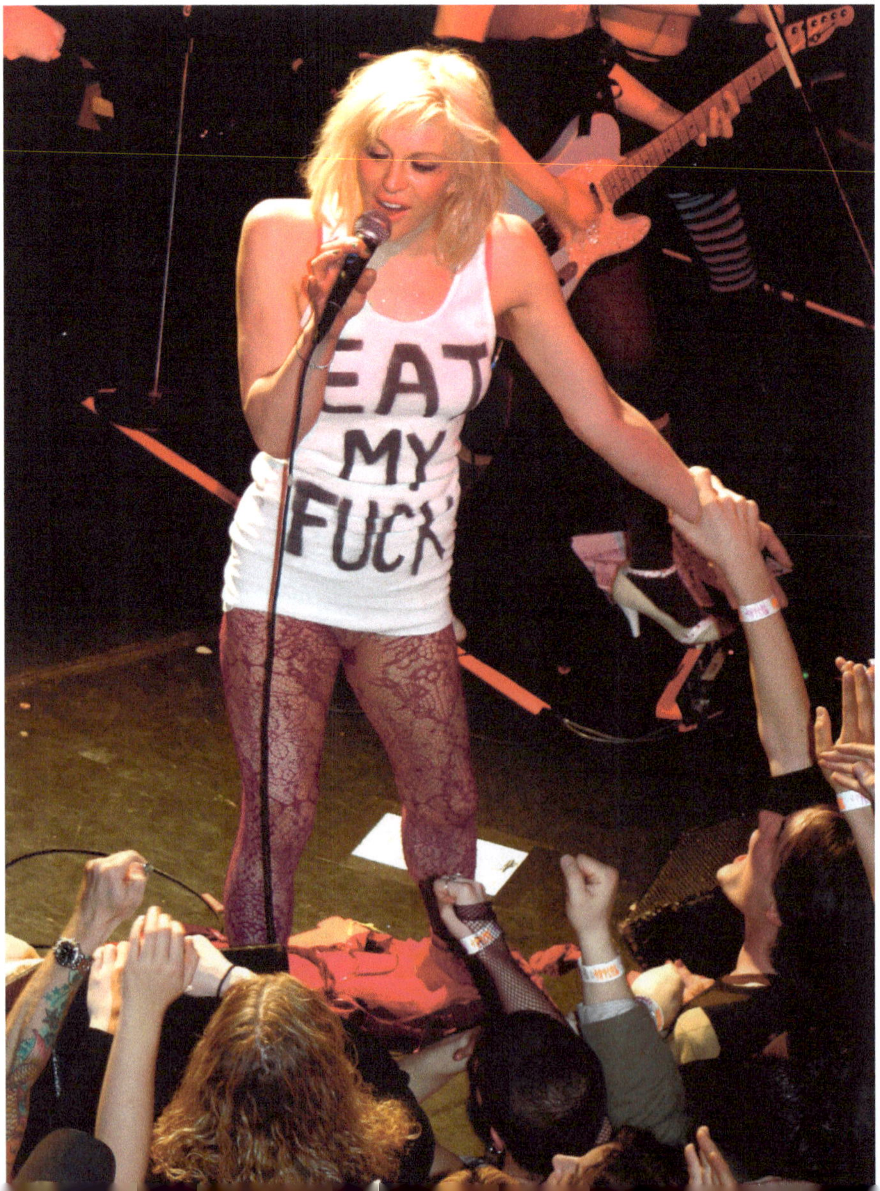

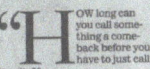

COUNTERPUNCH
As indie band struggles, Love's act is wearing well

By Kevin Ausmus

"How long can you call something a comeback before you have to just call it quits?" Robert Hilburn posed this question at the start of his review of Courtney Love in San Diego ["Who Knew She Had a Cuddly Side?" Oct. 26]. From my bowl of Cheerios, I could not evade the double irony of this statement. How long indeed?

The review was published on the same day I was to do the final mix-down on a Neil Diamond song, recorded for an indie tribute compilation to be released early next year. It's a big step for my band, the Desperation Squad. In our 20-plus years, this song, a cover, represents the first time we will receive even (modest) national distribution of our product.

All the other accoutrements of fame — the airplay, the sponsorship, the cash advances — are still out there in million-to-one land, a place where, if your on-call job stops contacting you for two weeks, the life raft starts to take on a little more water, and stress and distraction become part and parcel of the insurmountable odds you live by every day.

In show business, the bigger you are, like Love, certainly the harder you will fall. But your fall will at least be, at various times, softened by whatever celebrity cachet you've managed to build up for yourself. Courtney Love, even in free fall, is still a compelling media figure. And that in itself will keep generating additional chances for her.

But for those with no cachet, living dirt-poor in a vain attempt to somehow grasp the holy grail of mainstream success is considered, well, wholly pathetic. There's no bronze medal for hanging in there, for coming close.

The true artist, however, knows that as long as there is a flicker of light emanating from the candle, that is reason enough to stay the course. But if you want to compete in the big time, you've got to have some kind of game. Everyone knows that. Resilience is OK; free fall is better.

And that's where Courtney, whom I have never met, did Desperation Squad a great favor. The night after her arrest in New York last spring, Love went on stage at the Bowery with a defiant three-word message on her shirt that included an obscenity. The media noticed this and reported it.

Here's the deal: That's our foul shirt. We handmade it on my bass player Laura's back patio. Suddenly, it's on dozens of websites, all over television and in magazine spreads. Our stupid shirt. From a San Gabriel Valley back patio to the Bowery, though how Love got it I can only guess. I sold a couple to a hip clothes boutique on Cahuenga once, but that was in 2002.

I guarantee you this: That's a D-Squad shirt, flung out there in the media landscape like a big old stinking cigar ad. And I was determined to cash in!

I contacted every media outlet that ran the shirt photo, and Hilburn too, and told them, "Hey, that's our shirt," less to crow about it than to train a spotlight on my band. I got zero response.

I know why. It's not the message but the messenger. With no agent, manager, publicist, with no celebrity cachet, my claims of artistic triumph elicited not a shred of interest from the media, not even a "You must be lying." Had I the clairvoyant panache to see it coming, I might have sent out a news release the week before that said, "Courtney Love to Have Nervous Breakdown in D-Squad Shirt." And even that might not have helped.

In a business of celebrity cachet and savvy promotional sticks, it is unavoidable that worthy artists fall through the cracks. But Hilburn and other journalists should be advised that "calling it quits" is rarely a viable option, even through a lifetime of obscurity.

I remain optimistic. One more rock star wears my shirt and I get a free sandwich at my local deli!

Kevin Ausmus works alternately as a driver, a freelance writer and a singer for the band Desperation Squad, which plays every fourth Saturday at 51 Buckingham in Pomona. He lives in Claremont.

Counterpunch

Counterpunch is a weekly feature designed to let readers respond to reviews or stories about entertainment and the arts. Please send proposals to: Counterpunch, Calendar, Los Angeles Times, 202 W. 1st St., Los Angeles, CA 90012. Or Fax: (213) 237-7630. Or e-mail: calendar@latimes.com. Important: Include full name, address and phone number. Please do not exceed 600 words. We appreciate all proposals and regret that we cannot respond to each.

Mr. P penned an insightful "Counterpunch" column for the L.A. Times, in response to a Courtney Love live review by longtime Times rock critic Robert Hilburn, entitled "As Indie Band Struggles, Love's Act Is Wearing Well." In it, Mr. P touches on the nature of celebrity, resilience and free fall, and the role of the press in all of it. The piece ended with the line, "One more celebrity wears our shirt, I get a free sandwich at my local deli."

The affair was neatly summed up by Joe Piasecki, in the Pasadena Weekly's "Shirt Famous, Band Nowhere" piece. Piasecki and Kevin Urich, editor of the Weekly, were friends with Laura and big D-Squad fans. Mr. P was even a contributing writer for Pasadena Weekly at the time.

Another article was published the following summer, writing about Love and the shirt from a slightly different perspective, in Mat Gleason's Coagula magazine. This article put the questions to the art world itself: What constitutes fame? What is a breakthrough work? What is mass recognition?

Courtney Love had achieved a level of success that drew attention to her every move. And one of those moves was made in a Desperation Squad shirt.

Where in the world could you find Desperation Squad rubbing elbows with the likes of porn stars, Tony award winners, trannies, professional wrestlers, reality show survivors, sitcom comediennes, voluptuous go-go dancers, celebrity bloggers and an openly gay talk show host? That would be "Queer Edge with Jack E. Jett", a campy, taste-challenged variety show that aired on the now-defunct Q television network in 2005.

Steve Jones, the former lead singer of the Unforgiven, was a producer and writer on "Queer Edge" and realized right away that the band's outrageous antics matched up well with the irreverent Jett and his sidekick, former Rhino Bucket drummer Jackie Enx.

Desperation Squad was asked to be the "house band" for a full week of shows, which included playing original material and providing "bumpers" in between commercial breaks. This proved to be tricky. Though J.P. Maramba had come on board to replace Laura, the band repertoire at that time was scarcely enough to get through one

show. Nevertheless, D-Squad jumped in enthusiastically.

The shooting schedule called for three "live" shows on Monday, Tuesday and Wednesday. The Thursday and Friday shows were pre-taped on Monday and Tuesday mornings respectively. This meant that the messy "Me and My Drug Problem" would be the band's introduction to the "Queer Edge" universe and as "edgy" as the show was, Mr. P was worried it would be too much and they would get bounced from the program.

What transpired was a brazen and shameless performance that caused a stunned and inspired Jack E. Jett to leap out of his chair and run over to lick the chocolate syrup off Mr. P's chest, while assuring his audience that Mr. P would certainly be going to hell.

Another surprise was how the band was handled by the "Queer Edge" staff. D-Squad was used to playing live gigs where no one cared if you showed up or not. But on "Queer Edge" everyone involved in the show was incredibly supportive. They all had the attitude that every day something great was going to happen.

Along the way the band met a wide potpourri of Hollywood celebs from actress Kim Coles, porn star Joanna Angel, the flamboyant dresser Bobby Trendy all the way to the super-hunky award-winning Alan Cumming.

Desperation Squad performed seven songs on "Queer Edge" - "Drug Problem", "Band", "Jello Ball", "Taco Truck", "Best Ass", "Your Girlfriend's Ugly", and "Girl With A Car" (because Steve Jones really wanted them to play it), while trying to deflect the mild ribbing given to them by Jett (who apparently was less than impressed with Panda Man's body odor).

On the last day of shooting, Panda Man sat on the couch for "Queer Edge's" end of the show sketch "What Have We Learned?", where he gave Jett the "Superqueer" t-shirt, the one Bob he had worn for the Fillmore show, and a Naked Panda Man clock.

Making Rock and Roll Crazy Again

by Danny Horgan

It was August 2nd, 2006, and like any good suburban American family, my household was gathered around the TV in our living room to watch network television. This night's pick was NBC's new reality show "America's Got Talent", a series that gave everyday people a chance to show off their performing abilities on a national stage while competing for a one-million-dollar grand prize.

I was 16 at the time, and my life could not have been more straight and narrow. I was a straight A student who studied grammar for fun. Anyone who didn't live a disciplined and rule-abiding life, I thought, had it all wrong.

So when a band called Desperation Squad abrasively introduced themselves on America's Got Talent, my first reaction was to roll my eyes. Were these guys serious?

But when Desperation Squad proclaimed that rock and roll in America had "gone down the toilet," my skepticism turned to excitement. Regardless of the band's talent, it was clear they would be bringing a grenade launcher of energy as they took that night's biggest stage in the world. And their promise to "make rock and roll crazy again" would be a big one to live up to with millions of eyes watching.

Regis Philbin, the show's famous host, introduced the Southern California band:

"Well, they certainly are passionate, but are they talented? Anything can happen on this stage right now. Here they are singing, 'Band', it's Desperation Squad!"

In the blink of an eye, Desperation Squad

139

turned the America's Got Talent stage into a fucking zoo. Mr. P jumped up and down chanting vocals while drummer Ian Crosstown slammed his drums violently in the background. The cameras cut to a confused crowd and the show's perturbed judges while the song hit its first verse, but Mr. P immediately re-commanded attention with his animated stage presence.

Mr. P ran to the judges table, screamed "we're a good band!" and hit one of the check buttons. He then proceeded to yell "we're a bad band!" and hit one of the X buttons, confusing everyone in the crowd. He repeated the lyrics and button mashing one more time, then ran back on stage as the judges sat still, completely shocked by what they'd just seen.

At this point it started to become clear what Desperation Squad was doing. This was the craziness that rock and roll had lost. This was the type of wild, anarchic fun missing from modern music. This was the type of shit that would bring rock and roll back out from the toilet. Riding the momentum of energy, Desperation Squad guitarist Bob Jones pulled off a masterclass guitar solo while Mr. P ran back on stage, only to briefly disappear from the camera's view. When he reemerged seconds later, he was wearing a panda mask on his head, putting an exclamation point on the bedlam the band brought to the stage. The song came to a close, and I told my sister that Desperation Squad was my new favorite band.

The following morning I went on Myspace.com, at the time the world's social networking site of choice, to see if I could find out more the insane band I'd seen the night before. I found their page, and it turned out I wasn't the only new fan Desperation Squad had made. The band's profile was flooded with hundreds of comments from people around the world telling them how much they kicked ass. The insanity that took place the previous night on national TV was the fire music had been missing for years. And Desperation Squad were heroes for bringing it back. I left my own fan comment and proceeded to listen to every one of the band's songs I could find online.

I continued to follow the band in the coming years. Their song "Welcome to the Drunkfest" became my morning soundtrack on the way to school, and I repeatedly watched video of their live shows online. The music obviously had an impact on me because by 2008, I was fronting my own band, doing my part in creating

Backstage

the same type of fun and chaos I had seen from Desperation Squad on NBC.

What's interesting, though, is that even as mainstream music veers further and further away from rule-breaking rock and roll, the fire is still burning, even if it's not overly apparent. Brandy, the America's Got Talent judge who publicly said she had nothing to do with Desperation Squad being on the show, had originally put the band through an untelevised preliminary round, giving them the TV spot. She may not have wanted to admit it, but the pop star actually liked the band.

Desperation Squad is one of the few bands in the world that ever brought real rock and roll to primetime national television. And while the music industry continues to shy away from bands looking to stir up the pot, true rock fans can be proud that for one night in 2006 -- on the biggest stage in the world -- rock and roll was made crazy again.

In less than a year, Desperation Squad had appeared twice on national television. Panda Man had cavorted on camera with Regis Philbin and also Philbin's queer counterpart, Jack E. Jett.

As a YouTube clip of the "America's Got Talent" appearance went viral, the band was slammed mercilessly in the comments, with 90 percent of the hatred directed solely at Mr. P for being the worst singer of any band in the history of music. The slurs were venomous but not without their twisted charm - "Abortion Poster Child" was Mr. P's favorite.

Over time, D-Squad would occasionally hear from newly converted fans - especially when "America's Got Talent" was broadcast overseas. The most ecstatic by far was a teenaged journalist from Boston, Dan Horgan, who assured the band that their performance on TV had changed his life.

Two other young fans were the Gleason brothers, who had first seen D-Squad at a 51 Buckingham show with the Radioactive Chickenheads. The Gleason brothers band, The McDaniels, a sort of demented punk Osmond Brothers, were on the bill at D-Squad's first post-AGT gig at the California

Institute of Abnormal Arts (CIA), a show which proved how little the band's fortunes had changed. Barely two weeks after being comped hotel rooms and free meals paid for by a television network, D-Squad was being chewed out by an ambivalent ticket taker over a miscommunication about the guest list.

A mini-tour that included some northern California show was equally disastrous. The lowlight was a gig at San Jose's preeminent punk showcase the Blank Club, where the band was shut down in the middle of their set by the bartender/manager shortly after they hit the final note of "Taco Truck" because, as he told Mr. P, "I saw whipped cream and chocolate syrup and I didn't want to clean it up. I'm not a janitor." Retro punk fliers featuring Fear and Black Flag posted all over the

venue and Desperation Squad was shut down for being too messy.

But the tour ended well, with a last-minute show with old ISW buddy Count Dante and the Black Dragon Fighting Society at the Caravan in San Jose which, coincidentally, was just one block down the street from the Blank Club.

The final stop on the tour was at the LiPo Cocktail Lounge in San Francisco, with Stoo Odom of the Graves Brothers Deluxe. The GBD had met up with D-Squad several years earlier at Spaceland and got so rowdy during the Panda Man/Bikini Girl wrestling match, they got tossed out of a venue they had just played. The GBD just assumed that D-Squad caused violent audience reactions everywhere they went. At the LiPo, it was a free-for-all, with D-Squad besieged all night by an audience that thought they were asking for it.

It was hard to fathom. Desperation Squad had always been a band that inspired good times. That was their motto upon resurrection - "FUN IS BACK". In 2007 the band found themselves continually swept up into a vortex of violence - a Vietnam vet who thinks Mr. P is desecrating the American flag on stage and attacks him; a benefit for a women's roller derby team turns into a brawl between teammates; in the desert, Mr. P has to face down a drunken sociopath in order to recover his blow-up doll.

The band was displeased with the continual distracting antics, but they were developing no new material. The antics would stay and rarely would D-Squad play a show in peace.

Call it the "Taco Truck" effect.

Photo by Kayleigh Skajem

Virtually from the start "Taco Truck" was a crowd favorite, an upbeat number that sagely anticipated the coming food truck craze that would sweep through Los Angeles in the mid-00's. After playing the Fillmore at "Homomania", it was plainly obvious to all concerned the tortilla-throwing had to stay in the act.

Fans loved the tortilla-throwing; club owners loathed it. Before long "Taco Truck" easily became the most controversial song they had every played, one certain to land them in hot water and quite likely have the band shut down and never invited back. Desperation Squad was even wearing out their welcome at places like The Press Restaurant in Claremont, who stopped booking them.

Amid this brouhaha came a small ray of hope. Kevin Lyman, after six years, had offered the band a slot on the 2007 Warped Tour – for one gig, in Pomona.

In early June, a band profile appeared in the Inland Empire Weekly titled "You Guys Are Fags!", a sympathetic recap of the band's recent troubles, which ended with Mr. P warning indie punk this was the last chance they had to appreciate the band or they were going to "go Largo" (a reference to the trendy Hollywood club D-Squad had no chance of getting booked at).

Not Just Another Warped Tour
In its 13th year, 13 reasons to go back

6. THE GODDAMN DESPERATION SQUAD!

Our loyal readers remember this featured act a couple weeks back in the Weekly's Local Music Issue. But here's a total reminder that longtime Pomona panda-laden punks Desperation Squad will fight for their right to party (and for your approval or disdain) at this exclusive Warped '07 appearance. "Cheerleaders and Beer," anyone?

145

They also scored a profile in the Skratch Magazine Warped Tour preview where Mr. P revealed the difference between being a loser band and being the loser band (pass off all the bad things that happen like they are the greatest things that ever happened), belittled "comedy rock" bands, and made a bold prediction that D-Squad would "blow out" all the other bands on the Warped Tour.

But their biggest coup was scoring an exclusive interview with the Warped Tour pit reporter, who was based on the east coast. A band interview was completed via email with Mr. P editing the responses himself. The rambling interview discussed a number of light-hearted topics, from recent travails and TV appearances to the Rock and Roll Mayor campaign and their ties to Kevin Lyman. Several passages today seem eerily prescient. One was the pit reporter's admonition, "Should be pretty crazy, so check it out!". Another was Mr. P's promise there would be "tortillas, lots of tortillas."

Mr. P deliberately inserted at the beginning of the interview, a thought about the band that had been rolling around in his head for several years as D-Squad seemingly spun its wheels in spectacular fashion and no one really seemed to know what to think of them.

> "Many people mistake us for a rock and roll band. It's not true. We're an art collective."

The interview was posted online the day before the show. The day after the show, the interview was taken off the Warped Tour website, never to reappear. What could have possibly have happened in the interim? How bad could the gig have been that Desperation Squad would never again to be asked to play a show on any indie circuit, punk or otherwise?

**DESPERATION SQUAD
HURLEY STAGE 8:00**

It became known as the "Riot Gig" and to the casual observer Mr. P was a remorseless instigator. It's true that once the bottles and trash started flying he did nothing to stop it, but that had more to do with the fact it was the Warped Tour, Punk Rock Summer Camp. Putting the brakes on free expression would have gone against long-held principles. Plus, no one was getting hurt.

In truth, the events of June 29, 2007, Desperation Squad's official expulsion from the modern music scene, were a perfect storm of random unrelated events, no one of which could cause a riot on its own, but together produced a spectacular uprising that quickly spun out of control.

D-Squad was scheduled for an early evening set on the Hurley.com stage. Mr. P arrived at the stage to find a solid 200 entertainment-starved kids milling about and went to the front of the stage to engage with them and keep them entertained until the show started. Having a surplus of tortillas at his disposal, he started playfully tossing them to the crowd, along with some demo CDs.

The reaction to the tortilla-flinging was fairly predictable. The kids, nearly all of whom had endured a full day in the heat, started throwing them back, along with water bottles, empty or otherwise. By the time the rest of the band arrived, the stage was already littered with a great deal of trash, and the gig had not even started.

When D-Squad began their set, all hell broke loose. Bottles, food,

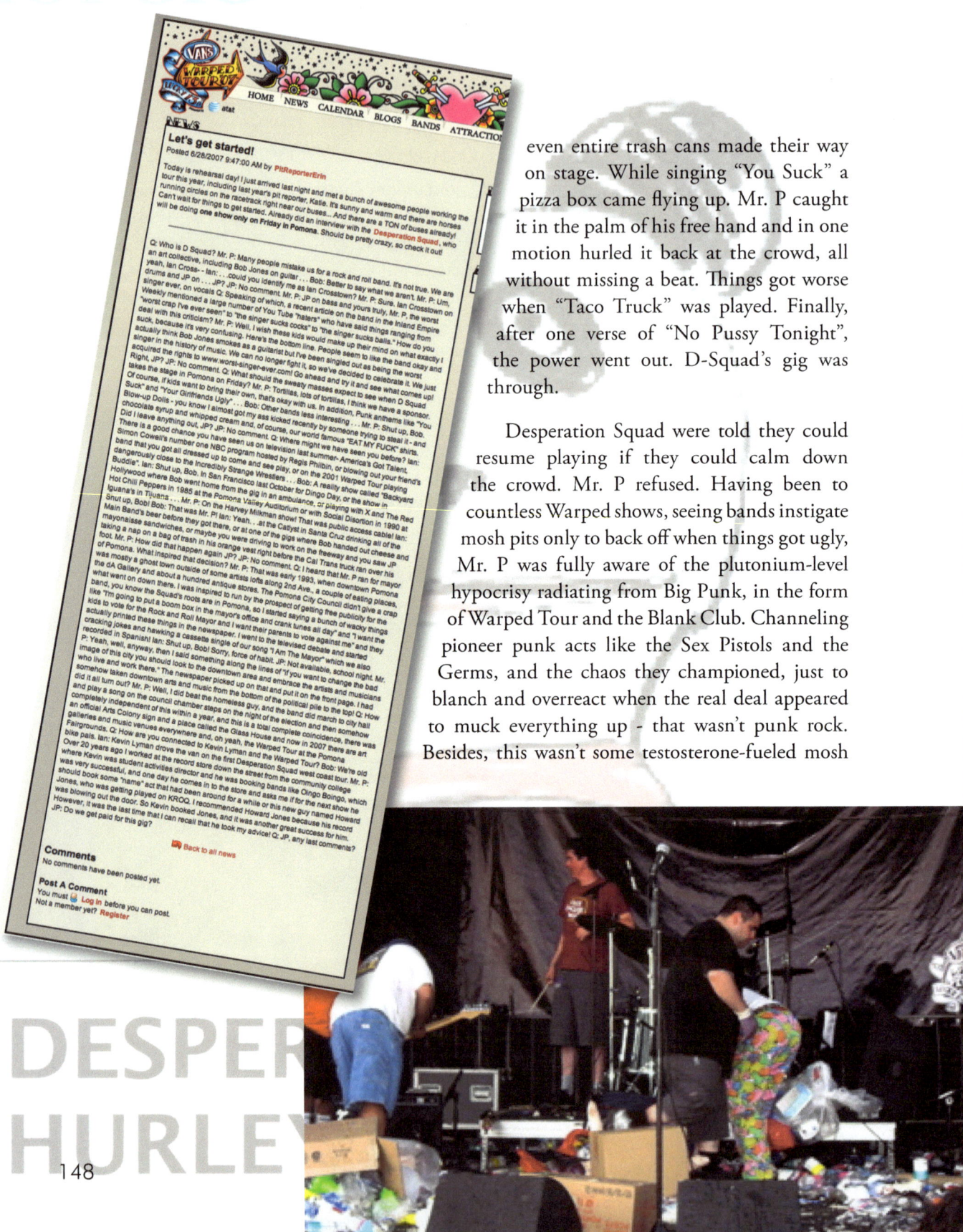

even entire trash cans made their way on stage. While singing "You Suck" a pizza box came flying up. Mr. P caught it in the palm of his free hand and in one motion hurled it back at the crowd, all without missing a beat. Things got worse when "Taco Truck" was played. Finally, after one verse of "No Pussy Tonight", the power went out. D-Squad's gig was through.

Desperation Squad were told they could resume playing if they could calm down the crowd. Mr. P refused. Having been to countless Warped shows, seeing bands instigate mosh pits only to back off when things got ugly, Mr. P was fully aware of the plutonium-level hypocrisy radiating from Big Punk, in the form of Warped Tour and the Blank Club. Channeling pioneer punk acts like the Sex Pistols and the Germs, and the chaos they championed, just to blanch and overreact when the real deal appeared to muck everything up - that wasn't punk rock. Besides, this wasn't some testosterone-fueled mosh

Mr. P in action at Warped

pit, it was a fairly resourceful "trash" riot - plastic bottles and clumps of grass - set in motion by the punk version of a soccer pitch "own goal". The riot happened because of a scheduling fuck-up.

There were 200 sun-stroked kids huddled up with great anticipation at the *Hurley.com* Stage to see Escape the Fate, a hugely popular post-hardcore band, when Mr. P walked on stage. The kids had no idea that Escape the Fate was clear across on the other side of the park on the *Hurley Stage*. Mr. P had no idea they were waiting to see Escape the Fate. He truly thought playing a bigger stage brought with it a bigger profile show. The stage confusion proved consequential. Both Mr. P and the kids got fooled. Both paid the price - the kids missed out on their favorite band and Mr. P took D-Squad to the brink of being blacklisted. And it was stunningly well-documented.

No less than four media outlets were there to observe and photograph the madness. Besides Nate Solis and Orlando Pina of SmashedChair.com, who dutifully reported the carnage on their website, there was Waleed Rashidi from the Inland Empire Weekly, who had trumped up the band's appearance in the mag's Warped Tour preview. Also present was Kevin Bronson, the L.A. Times Buzz Bands blogger. Rashidi and Bronson both reviewed the show for their publications. Notably absent from the coverage was the Warped Tour Pit Report, showing that there was apparently some rock and roll news unfit to print.

After the 2001 Warped Tour, some had thought D-Squad was blacklisted from the indie punk scene. After the Riot Gig, it was no longer a conspiratorial thought.

Of all bands in the history of rock and roll, it just happened that Desperation Squad was the one deemed "too punk" for the largest profile and successful punk rock music tour of all time. For their first gig after proclaiming themselves an "art collective", it certainly provided food for thought.

Desperation Squad's Era of Bad Feeling wasn't done quite yet. The McDaniels prevailed upon the band to headline a show at Hogue Barmichaels in Newport Beach. Despite the anathema of being a pre-sale gig, D-Squad agreed to it since it was an all-ages show that would be attended primarily by teenagers. By this time, The McDaniels had developed a bit of a troublemaking reputation themselves and D-Squad had hoped to mitigate controversy by placing "Taco Truck" at the end of their set. Perhaps, this time, D-Squad would not have the plug pulled on them. Plus, amazingly, they had managed to sell close to 50 pre-sale tickets. It looked to be a well-attended, feisty yet manageable show.

A spirited line-up of punky kid bands played throughout the day, with plenty of audience interaction. The McDaniels made sure most of their crowd stuck around to see the D-Squad, and for most of their set, the band reveled in their new-found adulation. At one point, during "Drug Problem", two teenaged girls jumped on stage and helped rub chocolate syrup on Mr. P's chest.

Despite the positive response, in the end, Desperation Squad could not avoid running afoul of the club and its uptight promoters and staff. The moment tortillas began to fly

during "Taco Truck" thuggish security personnel came on stage and stopped the show, before even Mr. P could change into Panda Man. They then threw everybody out.

It got worse. After the show, the promoters strongly suggested their old rundown P.A. and stage equipment had been severely damaged and were hounding Mr. P, demanding his drivers license ID just in case they found him liable. Realizing this, Mr. P marched back into the club and, at great physical risk (bouncers shadowed him the entire time), conducted a post-gig sound check to make sure every single microphone and monitor was functioning at full capacity.

When he finally emerged from the club, he was greeted by a cheering throng of teen supporters. In a loud voice, Mr. P pointedly discredited the promoters and warned them not to attempt to hold him responsible for any supposed damage. The club responded by calling the police. It may have been a bluff, but Mr. P hightailed it out of there anyway.

Shortly after this show, J.P. retired from the band, leaving D-Squad once again without a bass player. The last year had been rough. It was one thing to live up to punk ideals; it was yet another thing to live up to them and be despised and blacklisted from everywhere you played.

Bob Calhoun, leader of Count Dante and the Black Dragon Society and longtime voice of the Incredibly Strange Wrestlers, was also a prolific writer whose 2008 memoir, **"Beer, Blood & Cornmeal: Seven Years of Incredibly Strange Wrestling"** had a nice surprise in it for Desperation Squad. In the book, he identifies D-Squad as "the best act on the entire 2001 Warped Tour", a rather stunning proclamation, all things considered. Calhoun's high praise for the band was topped in "Beer, Blood & Cornmeal's" entertaining color photo section. The first several pages show action shots of Count Dante and other popular members of the ISW like El Pollo Diablo, The Poontangler and The Ladies Man. Then, a shot for the ages: Panda Man at the Fillmore.

It's a full page shot taken by Rog Franklin that makes the case, at that very moment in time, Desperation Squad was the hottest band on the planet. Arms outstretched like a triumphant wrestler, Panda Man is Adonis in chocolate syrup, a junior panda adorning a leopard-print thong, a wry smile emanating from the disembodied mask.

This combination of visual power and fabled location perfectly encapsulated Warped Tour-era Desperation Squad. Several more pages with band pictures followed the Panda

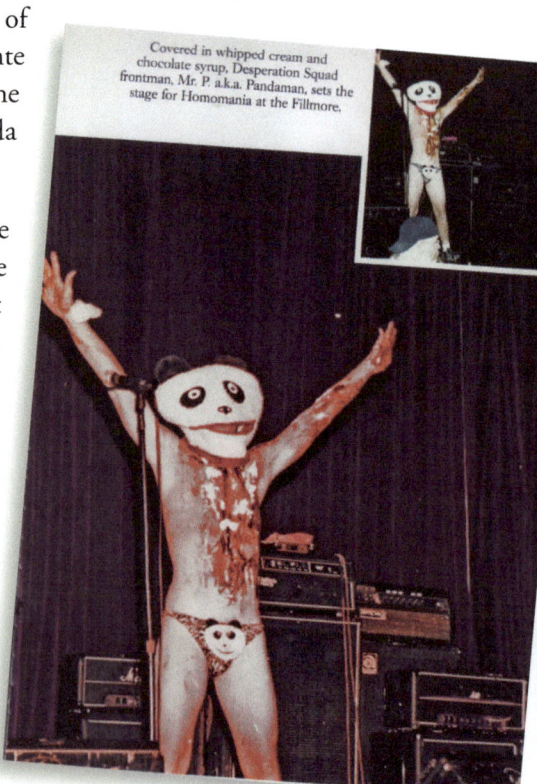

Covered in whipped cream and chocolate syrup, Desperation Squad frontman, Mr. P. a.k.a. Pandaman, sets the stage for Homomania at the Fillmore.

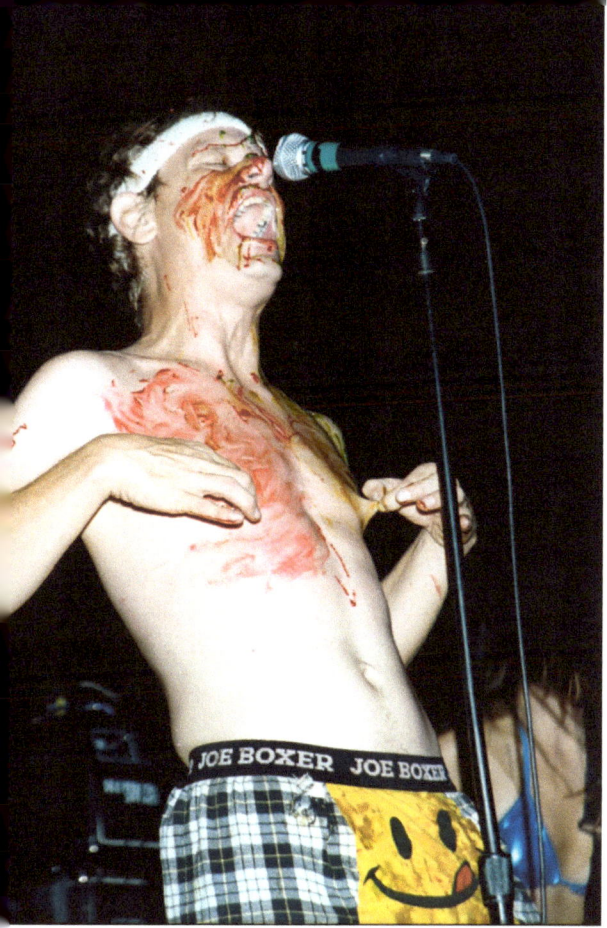

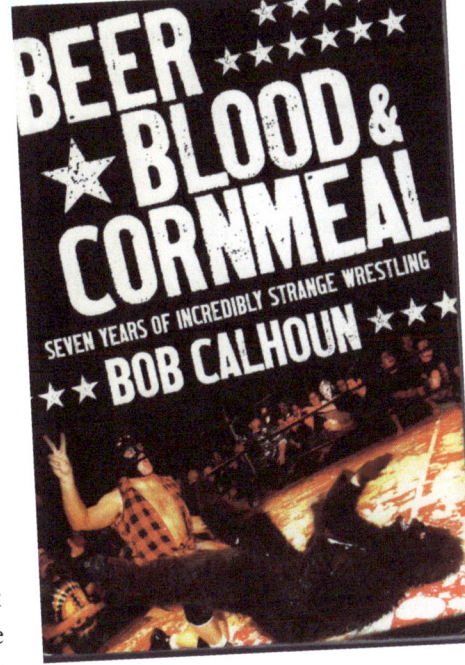

Man shot, including one of notorious punk troublemakers The Dwarves and even a second one of Mr. P, pinching his nipples during "Me and My Drug Problem".

Calhoun invited the band up to play the book release party, along with the Angry Amputees. Laura was recruited to play bass. It was a nice shot in the arm for a band that had stopped playing after J.P. had left the band.

25 years of being woefully neglected as a band, Desperation Squad had consistently won the battle in a different arena, where irreverent outrage counted for something. Photo editors loved the Desperation Squad. It's been a consistently overlooked quality of the band, especially the Millennial Squad, winning the coveted spots in newspaper and magazine photo layouts.

You have to hand it to Panda Man. He knows how to get attention. He's always a good time.

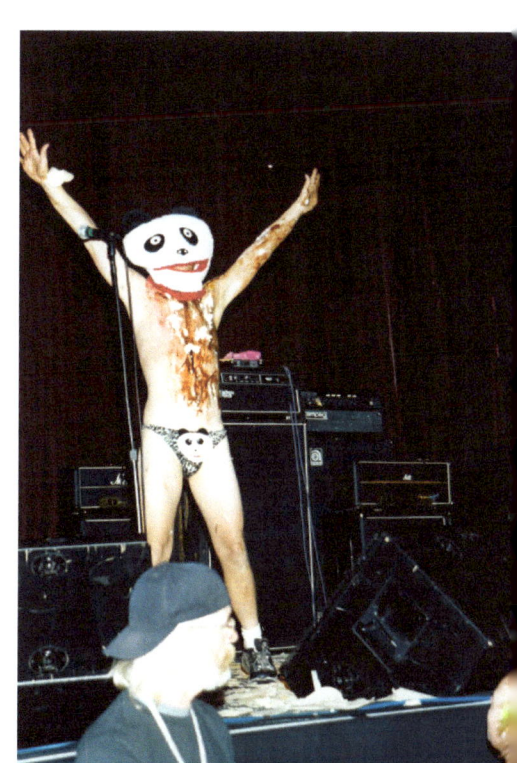

Mr. P became a writer for the Inland Empire Weekly in September 2007. He became a staff writer early in 2008, writing mostly news stories and the occasional feature, and **traveled to Japan to cover the World Baseball Classic,** Major League Baseball's version of the World Cup.

Baseball always interested Mr. P, and when he saw that there was a Tokyo round in the World Baseball Classic, he immediately applied for a media pass, bought a ticket, and he was off.

The "Tokyo Round" consisted of one week of exhibition games involving the international teams - Japan, South Korea, China, and Chinese Taipei - and participating Japan League teams, like the hometown Yomiuri Giants, who played in the Tokyo Dome, where the tournament was held. The second week was the tournament itself, with a round-robin elimination and championship game.

Mr. P visited with friends he had met while working at an ESL school in Covina, but spent most of his time at the Tokyo Dome watching baseball as an officially credentialed corespondent, hanging out in his seat in the Tokyo Dome press box, or watching the official WBC press conference downstairs after the game.

Mr. P met many of the Japanese Press Corp beat writers, a few of them Americans who wrote for the Japanese newspaper English web sites. Almost upon arrival at the Tokyo

Dome, Mr. P was taken under the wing of Fumihiro Fujisawa, "Fu-Chan" to all his friends, President of the American Association of Baseball Research.

Of all the players Mr. P saw, one stood out, a first baseman for the Japan national team, and member of the Yomiuri Giants, Michihiro Ogasawara, or as Giants fans loudly chanted every time he came up to bat – "O-GA-SA-WARA"! and then clap their hands in time, over and over, "O-GA-SA-WARA". The highlight of the entire trip was the final night, after South Korea delivered a crushing defeat to Japan to win the Tokyo Round, Mr. P sat at the press conference and asked all of the English language questions, grilling the Japan national team manager on his game strategy.

Mr. P arrived home amidst tragic circumstances. During the Japan visit, his older brother Regi passed away suddenly at home. To add to the grieving, the IE Weekly abruptly backed off Mr. P's WBC story, even as the championship game - held at Dodger Stadium - was a rematch of the Tokyo Round combatants, Japan and South Korea. There would be no award-winning cover story for Mr. P, just a funeral and a pink slip.

From Japan, Fu-Chan reached out to Mr. P to write an article for his AABR magazine, *Ballpark*. Mr. P already knew his subject - the popular first baseman for the Japan National Team and Yomiuri Giants.

Mr. P couldn't shake the "O-GA-SA-WARA" chant from his head. It stayed with him for weeks, until Ian found some YouTube video of the

chant and learned the drum pattern. "Ogasawara" the song was born.

Now down to a trio, Desperation Squad - Mr. P, Ian and Bob - went to Jon Crawford's Interstellar studio (which happened to be Mike Gonzales' old studio, where they recorded "This is Our Demo"), and recorded "Ogasawara". This marked the first collaboration between D-Squad and Crawford, who shared the bill with the band at the Rock Wars back in 1984 as a member of the Dash. The band had also played with Moonwash Symphony at Munchies in the early 90s.

The sound was dynamite. "Ogasawara" was Desperation Squad's first-ever iTunes release.

The next year was the inaugural screening of the "909 Film Festival" created by Eddie Gonzales, Mr. P's old buddy from Pitzer and former host of "Harvey Milkman", a Glendora-based public access cable show the band played on back in 2002.

D-Squad decided to film its first official music video since "Serious Love" to include at the festival. The video of "Ogasawara" is part-documentary, part-music video, part-Ian's backyard pool party, which included newly-arrived bass player Vidal Lepe and was filmed primarily by Steve Cormack, Laura's husband, and Laura herself, providing a festive atmosphere for the day long shoot.

Desperation Squad was named "Best Band - Pomona" in Inland Empire Magazine's year-end readers poll while "Ogasawara" was shown at the 909 Film Festival and was awarded the "International Prize" for spreading the Inland Empire name to such faraway places.

Caroline Collins brought the female singer back to Desperation Squad. She played a handful of gigs at the end of 2010 and into the new year. When she departed, Nicole Frazer was recruited to sit in at the Doll Hut, a show that, even by D-Squad drunk standards, was a doozy.

Shortly thereafter, Mr. P and Nicole formed a duo, the Boogie Sisters (after the Nixon's Revenge song of the same name), and performed at the Hip Kitty Open Mike Nights playing an eclectic array of cover songs like Neil Young's "Hold Back the Tears", Lady Gaga's "I Like It Rough" and a smashing version of The Veronica's "I'm A Revolution."

But new material was not being developed in either project. Desperation Squad had only new song to show for three years - Vidal's "Uckfay Ouyay" a high-energy number that had supplanted "Jello Ball" from the opening medley. It seemed as if Desperation Squad was at a crossroads.

One of the casualties of the many personnel changes during the 00s was Desperation Squad's recording output, which was sporadic but occasionally inspired.

In late 1999, a Citrus College recording arts student, Roy Zimpel, brought the band in for an ambitious project, a 12 song recording session, which included many old catalog tunes never recorded like "Looking Good" and "The Club". Among the other songs were "All Kinda People", a song penned during a wild road trip through Kansas City in 1990, the lyrics of which were written on a series of bar napkins; and "Sal Stine", the original "A-Side" to "Jello Ball", written by a 10-year old Mr. P. These recordings were never quite finished and were shelved when the band turned their attention to newer Warped Tour material.

In 2002 Mr. P met Rob Smith, a Pitzer College student who dropped out to become a recording engineer. Bringing in D-Squad as part of a UCLA Extension engineering class, Smith secured an afternoon at the legendary Sunset Gower Studios in Hollywood where the band cut Ian Carlson's "Stop Being A Dick", a notable session both for the ambiance and the fact that this would be the last recording by the Warped Tour unit of Mr. P, Hayes, Jones, Kovach and Carlson.

After Hayes' departure in 2005, D-Squad was approached by Curt Sautter, guitarist of The Relatives and old friend from the Green Door days, to submit a track for his Neil Diamond tribute CD, "A Little Bit Me, A Little Bit Neil". D-Squad chose "Brother Love's Traveling Salvation Show", which they recorded, with Laura on bass, at A to Z Studios in San Dimas. An amazing departure for the band - playing it straight - Sautter loved it and made it the leadoff track for the CD. The Boston Herald wrote "the 16-track is unfalteringly top-notch… starting with Desperation Squad's frolicking "Brother Love"… it's never been more obvious that

Diamond's songwriting transcends the dated arrangements with which we're most familiar."

After the America's Got Talent appearance, Desperation Squad went to a studio in Highland Park to record two songs, "Welcome to the Drunkfest" and "Cheerleaders and Beer" with J.P.'s brother as the engineer. Several months later, a separate session at Brian Gitting's house studio in Claremont netted "Isla Vista." These songs were issued as a three-song CD titled "Songs About College" and for one week in 2007 charted on KSPC's Hot 100. A video of "Isla Vista" recorded in Bob's garage was also posted on YouTube.

In 2008, Dan Horgan contacted Mr. P with the suggestion they should write and record a song about then-emerging Filipino boxing sensation Manny Pacquiao. The resulting "Running With The Pac-Man" was recorded at least four different times, twice at Brian Biddulph's studio (the band's latter-day rehearsal studio) with a young D-Squad fan Logan Barton playing bass; once in Bob Jones' garage, with old friend Hai Muradian laying down a flute track and new singer Caroline Collins providing backing vocals, and an unfinished track with Vidal Lepe on bass. None of these tracks were ever released officially, but the Muradian track wound up for a while on the band's MySpace page. Unfortunately, Pacquiao-mania failed to uplift the track into any kind of hit status, although it would eventually become a well-received live song during the band's Doll Hut shows.

In 2009, Wckr Spgt embarked on a tremendously ambitious project, "Smooth Sounds: Various Artists Play the Future Hits of Wckr Spgt." This was a departure from standard tribute CD's, as all tracks on the massive 40-track double-CD were new tracks previously unreleased by the band and, in fact, Spgt chose the songs in advance for bands to cover. D-Squad received "Look Forward To Dying Alone" which is notable mostly for the return of Dave Carpenter to play bass on the track. D-Squad contributed a strong set at the release show held in 2010 at the dA Center for the Arts in Pomona.

Lily Burk was a 17-year old high school senior running errands for her parents business in downtown L.A., when she was abducted and murdered, a story that gripped Los Angeles for weeks. Watching the news reports on TV, Mr. P was touchingly reminded of his own days as a teenager doing exactly the same thing, zipping around downtown running errands for his own parents business. He wrote the tribute ballad "Lily (You Will Not Be Forgotten)", which the band recorded with Vidal Lepe. It was the most stunning departure for Desperation Squad to date, with a magnificent guitar line from Bob Jones, vocals from Collins and the haunting refrain "Oh Lily, if I could switch places with you I would." The track was released on "See Who We Are" a compilation of Claremont-based bands issued on Hank Tracy's HT records in 2010.

Stopover in Wyoming

The "Ogasawara" video was a bit of a revelation to Desperation Squad. It was the rarest of things, a new work well-received enough to win an award at a local film festival. This prompted the band to look for other video opportunities.

There was plenty of leftover footage of Warped Tour 2001. Some of it - like the video shot inside the stretch limousine after being kicked off the bus - was compelling; other footage revealing, performance video of D-Squad in Las Vegas and Chicago (where the Tenacious D manager had seen them). Mr. P wanted to do something with film shot at a truck stop in Wyoming, where the band sends Bob Jones off to a fireworks stand and strands him there, talking shit about him the entire time.

It had all the elements of a hit, but upon inspection after 10 years, it was a big mess, really just three or four long meandering shots, Mr. P shaking the camera all over everywhere. The audio track was horrible, all noisy wind gusts and surface interference. The sound problems dictated that a quickie soundtrack be recorded, fittingly by the more current 2011 line-up with Mr. P, Ian, Bob and Vidal. In the end, it was a video project, 100 percent band-generated, that spanned eras. An appropriately tacky postscript was tagged on at the end, saving Bob the ignominy of being forever stranded by his band. It was a solid effort.

Called "Stopover In Wyoming" it screened at the 2011 909 Film Festival. But the important thing was not necessarily the film that was created, it was the moment that it preserved.

162

The context within which the film was created was this: the band was one full day back on the road after being kicked off their tour bus and was just embarking on a drive that would profoundly change every single member of the band. No one was spared the agony of the 2001 Warped Tour. It was a long, grueling hot hot summer. But in "Stopover in Wyoming" much of the true band drama conducted off-camera was still a day or two away, before they were at each other's throats on a hot and angry night at a Kansas City campground.

In "Stopover in Wyoming" it's all played for laughs. Let's just ditch this guy. Ha ha! How many bands have thought about that? Probably every single band that's ever toured. "Stopover in Wyoming" was Desperation Squad's gift to the touring band. It's a goofy, stupid video on its surface; peel away the layers of the onion and it's a remarkable look into the heart and soul of a band.

In November 2011, Mr. P received a phone call out of the blue from a woman named Karen Jewell, an intern for the Heidi & Frank show and she was calling to let Desperation Squad know that the radio program had received their demo CD and wanted to interview the band on an upcoming broadcast.

Mr. P was floored. Ian had indeed sent the radio hosts a CD - back in 2006, back when the pair was on KABC, an AM station in Los Angeles. In the years since, Heidi & Frank had been bounced from that station and in the not too distant future, they would replace the iconic Mark & Brian morning team on KLOS. Fittingly enough for D-Squad, the Heidi & Frank show was between those gigs and doing an internet show.

Desperation Squad would be included in an interview segment called "Should I Stay

Or Should I Go?" where bands plugged their music and were subjected to an audience vote.

It was a pretty hard gig to screw up, but D-Squad managed to do it anyway because they insisted on replacing the CD tunes that got them the gig – "Cheerleaders and Beer" and "Drunkfest", that J.P. had played on – with newer recordings of "You Suck" and "Taco Truck", which actually showed a precipitous drop in recording quality.

Heidi & Frank mostly did schtick instead of interviewing Mr. P who, for his part, pretended to be drunk on Schlitz Malt Liquor. After listening to the D-Squad songs, it was apparent that Heidi hated the band and that Frank kind of liked them. They split, and the listeners had their say. In the end, D-Squad prevailed by a 4-3 score, earning the right to say that for once in their life they weren't kicked off something.

For years, Desperation Squad had been rock and roll pariahs, routinely having the plug pulled on them. After Vidal Lepe joined the band, D-Squad made an effort to forge a new trail, trying to focus on the newer less confrontational material, "Ogasawara" "Pac-Man" "Lily" even the revived "Brother Love" but they ran smack into a brick wall - their own reputation as troublemakers which, for once, played out in their favor.

Vinny Malachi, a.k.a. "Vinny the Clown", played bass for The Yeastie Boys, an all-star conglomerate of Orange County punk players dressed up as clowns, playing punk covers with revised clown lyrics. The Yeastie Boys took a big shine to Desperation Squad, bringing them out to Anaheim for numerous shows at the Doll Hut, the O.C. punk rock shrine. For the first time in years, D-Squad was being welcomed with open arms at an esteemed venue that, true, had seen better days, but was also completely unfazed by its antics. It didn't matter, the Yeastie Boys made a much bigger mess, you couldn't top them. At the Doll Hut, D-Squad was encouraged to flail away, with tortillas flying and whipped cream spewing. Mr. P was sporting a new look - bright gold stretch pants three-sizes too small and an "I Heart Panda Man" t-shirt, again way too small. At the Doll Hut, it fit right in. D-Squad was all right with the Yeastie Boys.

It also provided a bit of a dilemma for the band, who had been trying in good faith to change its bad habits, catch on in a different type of venue. Like Tony Montana, the D-Squad kept getting sucked back in the racket. Then one night at the Doll Hut D-Squad was invited to play the big O.C. Punk Rock Picnic. Headlining the show was old friends, Jello Biafra and Fear.

The D-Squad gig was completely overshadowed by a

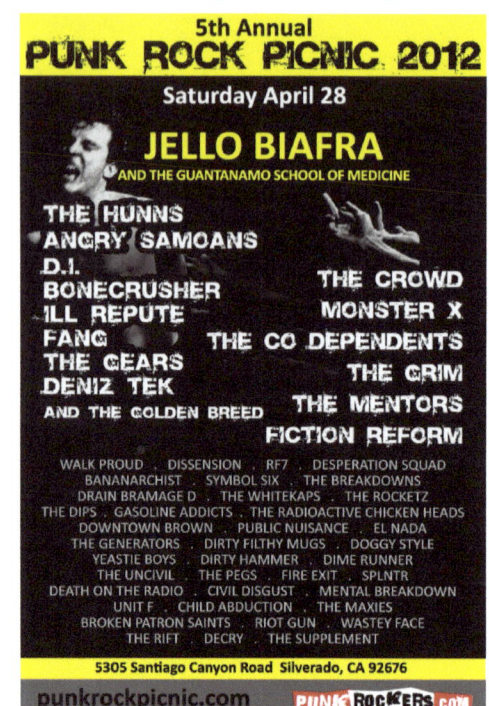

different show happening at one of their old haunts in Upland, where over the years every single Inland Empire band had played. This particular night in 2012, after a 25-year hiatus, The Unforgiven were back together again and on the bill at Stagecoach 2012. They were playing a warm-up show at the Black Watch Pub for all the diehards.

Undaunted, D-Squad proceeded to their big gig with high hopes. It was an all-day festival, with beer and close to 50 bands on a dozen different stages. That it was a heavy pre-sale ticket gig should have been the tip-off. Unless you were on a main stage at the Punk Rock Picnic, you got thrown into a field with tiny stages and barely working PAs.

Desperation Squad played before a small crowd of about 30 kids, including the first D-Squad show for Emma Waddington, Brian's daughter, who had heard the Nixon's Revenge recordings and brought them to her high school to share with her friends, starting a small Nixon's Revenge revival at Glendora High. With Emma were two of these newly-converted Nixon's Revenge devotees, Brandon Gould and Kyle Autrey. They were also seeing D-Squad for the first time.

D-Squad's performance at the Punk Rock Picnic was only average but the day was significant for another reason. Going all the way back to Warped Tour '01, Mr. P generally finished a gig looking like he had the shit beat out of him, occasionally reminiscent of G.G. Allin. Which of course was absurd

166

– Mr. P was only bathing himself in chocolate syrup and whipped cream – but many times it looked real and every once in a while, people would come up to Mr. P and express concern.

After going over to check out the Yeastie Boys, Mr. P wandered away from the stage and aroused the suspicion of two Orange County Sheriffs on patrol at the picnic, who motioned Mr. P over to talk to them. "Are you okay?" one of them asked. The cops were grilling Mr. P like he had had too much fun in the mosh pit and needed maybe to go the hospital. He could barely keep a straight face telling them sheepishly that the bruises and scars were actually cake icing and other food substances. The second cop bust out laughing, and the other one looked disgusted.

All the while, Alex Lopes, the son of John Ward, former resident of G5 and KSAK promotional flier figure, was several feet away with his camera, taking shots of the oddball confrontation, which ended amicably.

Later, the band headed out to the Black Watch to see the Unforgiven – Alan, John Henry Jones, Just Jones, Jay Lansford and a few "new members" to replace the ones who didn't want to play. It was a good show, attended by a huge contingent of Green Door old gang, with many unexpected encounters, like the one between Mr. P and Kevin Lyman, who had not spoken since the Riot Gig, five years earlier.

"Hey, P" said Lyman. "Hey, Kevin" said Mr. P.

Alan, Bruce, and Rod of Stratus with Nixon's Revenge songwriter Mike Levine at the American Legion, 2013

In May of 2013, D-Squad was contacted by Jeff Edison, a Harvey Mudd alum who was flying all the way from Belgium to go to his 25th year reunion. Would Desperation Squad want to play a special show for the occasion? Maybe play some of those old "Soul Cleanser" tunes, just have a good time?

For a show like this, it really had to be everyone - Waddington, Hayes, Laura, Becky, Givens - they all had to come back. It had to be a - gasp - reunion show. Which was okay. Everyone wanted to do it.

Very quickly another show was added, at the American Legion in Pomona. Word spread.

The American Legion show was much more than **a Desperation Squad reunion**, it was a reverential testimonial for the long forgotten crossed paths that constituted the groundwork for the band. M.J. Stevens opened the show with a bit of experimental guitar, accompanied by Brutus Chieftain laying down poetic riffs. Rod Curtis and Bruce Watkins were present, along with

Alan Waddington, the first time at least three Stratus members had been in the same room for years.

D-Squad blew through 30 years of hits, concentrating mostly on "Soul Cleanser" classics, with night's highlights being Curtis joining the band to play "That Thing" and, of course, Panda Man, resplendent in plastic clamshell bikini top and faux grass skirt.

There was lots of love the next night at Harvey Mudd as old college buddies reunited to enjoy the band they had spent many nights getting hammered to so many years before providing a perfect coda for their reunion weekend get together.

At the very end of the show, D-Squad played a cover version of "I Wanna Be Your Dog". It was the first time Desperation Squad had performed an Iggy Pop song and it reminded Mr. P of the time, two months before his own high school graduation, when Brian Waddington had suggested he buy a ticket to see Iggy Pop at the Santa Monica Civic. He glanced around, half-expecting to see Jill Emery in the crowd.

Among the attendees at the Legion show were soon-to-be Glendora High graduates Brandon Gould and Kyle Autrey. As seniors, they were allowed to place a quote in their yearbook, some profound statement that summed up their school years. On the same page where you could find citations from eminent philosophers like Plato and Emerson, as well as pop artists such as Fun and Eminem, was this obscure lyric submitted by Autrey:

In July 2014, a camera crew from the teen celebrity website Clevver.com was prowling the San Diego Convention Center, seeking out the more bizarre characters buzzing about Comic-Con. Clevver's young host, Erin Robinson, was trying to look past the usual suspects - Trekkies, zombies, anyone with a light saber - when she spotted a positively ridiculous looking freak sporting gold spandex pants, a humongous panda mask, and a skin tight t-shirt that read - "I (Heart) Panda Man".

"Hey, Panda Man," she shouted. "Would you like to be interviewed?"

Panda Man agreed to an interview, where he shook his butt, introduced "Panda Jr." and after revealing that his super power was singing, burst into a joyous rendition of "Taco Truck".

The resulting video, "Comic-Con Cosplay 2014: When Things Get Weird", posted on the YouTube Clevver Movies channel, garnered over 30,000 views and generated much love for Panda Man (a pointed contrast to the nasty comments he endured after "America's Got Talent"), with comments ranging from "Why is Panda Man not a thing?" to "Panda Man is love. Panda Man is life," and other similar praises.

CROSSED PATHS
Desperation Squad and the Age of Fortuitism

Art Show Opening
May 9, 2015

Space Gallery
250 West Second Street
Pomona, CA 91766

And look for the book from

www.pelekinesis.com

When it came to band memorabilia, Mr. P saved everything - concert tickets, band fliers, pictures, news clippings, phone numbers, original song lyrics, even gas receipts from the road. In 2013, he organized them into a huge computer file, labeled and listed in chronological order. It was a massive archive and, viewed from start to finish, told an amazing tale of a band and the various influences that preceded its formation.

One night, Nicole Frazer got a glimpse of this archive and quickly persuaded Mr. P that this was art show material. A few days later, Frazer and Mr. P met with Christina Franco-Long, whose Space Gallery in downtown Pomona was an ideal location for the show, not only because it was the band's original stomping ground but also because the Space was once Becky Hamm's art loft! Franco-Long, whose first Space exhibition featured the work of NY photographer Roberta Bayley, agreed to host the show.

So here we are.

What is Fortuitism?

The lines that are drawn upon the globe, the signals zipping around from one node to another, the paths that cross every day, the people we meet, and the sounds we hear - these are pieces of the world we live in, the world we embrace, and the decisions we make. How we interact with the pieces—which pieces we touch, which pieces touch us—determines how we see ourselves moving through life. Some decisions are out of our control. Some decisions are the lesser of two evils. How we use the results of these decisions are ours, and interact to shape who we are and how we live.

Fortuitism allows for a certain amount of serendipity and spontaneity to enter the art we create. The decisions we make are the signposts along the path.

Fortuitism is a different way to tell a story. Create art, save things, find a venue. You need not be famous or even enduring. Rock and roll is everyone's story. If you are fortuitous enough, you can tell your story in a way that makes it great art as well.

www.ingramcontent.com/pod-product-compliance
Lightning Source LLC
Chambersburg PA
CBHW041539220426
43663CB00003B/81